Finding
Thomas

Finding Thomas

John Fisher

HiP

HISTORY INTO PRINT

HISTORY INTO PRINT
56 Alcester Road,
Studley,
Warwickshire,
B80 7LG
www.history-into-print.com

Published by History Into Print 2013

A CIP catalogue record for this book is available from the British Library.

ISBN: 978-1-85858-346-4

Printed and bound
in Great Britain by 4edge Ltd.

Contents

Acknowledgements

To Christine for being so determined.

To Derdra at Birmingham for believing in me.

To my dear friend Janet for your ear and for your advice.

And to all who said to me you should write a book.

To my darling wife Diane, you inspire me,

and her darling sister, Jill, who inspired us all

with her courage and determination.

She endured her illness with great fortitude.

May her beautiful smile live on

in all who knew her.

Most of the important things in the world have been accomplished by people who have kept on trying when there seemed to be no hope at all.
— Dale Carnegie

ONE

Just Children

I AWOKE one September morning, rising from a urine sodden bed I shared with my younger brother Stephen. As usual I spent some time searching for the fleas jumping around on the bedclothes, knocking them to the floor and then scratching my head to relieve the itching of the head lice.

One of my favourite pastimes was to gather the head lice, ('bogies', as they became affectionately known) between my two thumbs and 'crack them', the bigger the 'bogie' the louder the crack. Then scuttle downstairs to an empty room whilst my mother slept upstairs, deep in sleep, recovering from the night before.

I recall it being a warm pleasant day with the sun shining outside and under normal circumstances within a normal family environment I guess I would have been looking forward to breakfast, a wash and then getting dressed for school. For most eight-year-olds this would I suppose be the normal process for the beginning of the day.

However, for me today was not to be a normal day. Today, certainly by the end of it was going to change my life forever. Today I was to embark on a journey that would last for over forty years. Whilst on this journey I would experience joy, confusion, contentment, heartache, the pain of bereavement and the most soul-destroying emotional rejection no child should ever be subjected to.

My name is John and this is my story.

This is me aged about two (on the next page).

In order to fully understand the catalyst for this particular day's events, let's go back to a time before I was born, to the early days of my family, to the days

when my mother and father first met. How they met and the circumstances surrounding that encounter I have never discovered. I assume as with most couples that those initial days and months of the relationship all went well.

Both my parents came from working class backgrounds, my father's parents both worked, my grandfather (Josiah,) a pipe layer and my grandmother (Lilly Elizabeth, born 1907) a factory worker. They lived in a modest council house on the Old Park Farm Estate in Dudley, West Midlands having moved from a house a mile or so away some time before.

My grandfather was born in October 1906 and strangely, but not uncommon, his father (my great grandfather) was also named John, born in 1875/6 he was I believe a coal miner/horse driver, my great grandmother Hannah was born in 1877 and my great, great grandmother Mary Ann born in 1826.

My grandfather had two brothers, one named Isaac, affectionately known as 'Ike' who was deaf and dumb and never married, he died fairly young so I'm told. The second brother was named 'Jack'. It seems to me that most of the male children in this side of the family at some point in the generation are christened or should I say named with a capital 'J'!

Jack had three sons Isaac, *Jack* and *Jim*! He also had two daughters Mary and Elsie, though I am somewhat surprised he didn't name them 'Janet' and 'Judith'! My grandfather also had two sisters, Sally and Beatrice, the latter having two sons, I bet you can't guess what she named them? James and Joseph – I kid you not!

On my mother's side I understand my grandfather (Luke) worked as a kiln hand (setter and drawer) in the pottery industry, he was born in 1891. My parents' marriage certificate identifies him as a labourer, so I assume he changed jobs at some point. My grandmother (Mary Ann) was born in 1893 and stayed at home to look after a large family, which was not uncommon all those years ago. They lived in a council house at Bluebell Road in Dudley, a house I have passed many times since leaving and have often thought of my time there. They were living there at the time my mother (Margaret Magdalene) was born in October 1935.

From the dates you can clearly establish the age difference between my grandmothers when they gave birth to my parents. My grandmother Fisher was 25 when my father was born in December 1932, and my grandmother Nicklin was 42 when she gave birth to my mother, her last child.

For the benefit of any budding genealogists in the family let me add my grandfather Nicklin's parents (my great grandparents) were named Joseph (born 1864) and Katherine (1868), and just to add a little more their parents (my great, great grandparents) were William (1822) and Hannah (1828). The gaps I'll let you fill in for yourself.

Anyway, during the years I spent growing up and the events that were to unfold it was clear to me that the two families did not get on. Listening and talking to various members of both families, there appeared to have been a division, born of resentment that my mother should not have married my father and visa versa.

This resentment and animosity was to play an important role in my life much later, to such an extent that it would have a profound effect on my emotional development through childhood and adolescence.

As I said, I don't know when my parents met or the circumstance, however, what I do know is that they married in September 1954 and I arrived January 1955. So I assume my father did the decent thing and married my mother after discovering she was pregnant.

My father's religion was Church of England and my mother's Catholic. They married at a Catholic church (The Church of Our Blessed Lady and St Thomas of Canterbury in Dudley), a requisite I presume that came from my mother's family. My father was 21 years of age, and my mother 19 at the time of their marriage. I was to be confirmed at the very same church some 11 years later.

My birth certificate identifies me as living with my mother's parents, at Bluebell Road, Priory Estate in Dudley and my father obviously moving in to complete the threesome.

My memories of Bluebell Road are quite vivid. It seemed a very busy household, my grandmother Mary, who I remember as being of average height and stout was always wearing a 'pinny' (pinafore). She did her cooking on the old fashioned 'black lead grate', with an open fire and pans hanging from a variety of hooks. That's all she ever seemed to be doing, apart from cleaning and washing.

Many folk used a lead based graphite polish to maintain these fireplaces, a practice unacceptable today, but this was what my grandmother used on the old kitchen range and fireplace. I can clearly remember her polishing it with a boot brush and then wiping down with a soft cloth to buff it up to the required sheen.

These days hardly anyone uses a cast iron range for cooking, or heating for that matter and most houses now have central heating with the fireplace forming a more decorative part of the room as the main focal point, those who might have such a cooking range would I suspect not use lead based polish.

How many of you, I wonder, also remember the old 'Cardinal' polish? My grandmother Nicklin often used this, as did my aunt Alice (her daughter, my mother's sister) to polish the concrete steps outside the front door. I remember the step becoming very slippery on occasions, I don't think you can get this particular polish so easily today.

I remember the house being fairly happy, no shouting, no upsets. Apart from my grandparents and parents, 'Uncle Ted' also lived there (my mother's brother).

Outside in the backyard there were a few chickens running around, I recall my grandfather chasing them around, catching one and wringing its neck. The poor thing would continue to run for a few seconds before dropping dead, my grandmother would then pluck it and prepare it for the oven.

Bluebell Road holds a particularly vivid memory for me of a dolls house that was kept in the corner of the downstairs toilet. It always seemed a decrepit old house that no one ever seemed to have played with, it must have been a left over from the girls in the family, my aunties. Every time I visited the toilet I experienced a creepy feeling surrounding that house.

My days at Bluebell Road were, as far as I can remember, happy ones.

Michael Graham was the next child to be born at Bluebell Road in April 1956. Unfortunately, Michael's time on this earth only lasted seven weeks. The information I have states that Michael's death was attributed to "suffocation due to overlaying", that is to say he was placed in bed with his parents and my mother lay on him and subsequently suffocated him.

Michael passed away on the 3rd June 1956. He is buried in a public grave at Dudley cemetery. The next child to be born at Bluebell Road was Stephen Robert, on 30th November 1957. It was to be two years before the first of two girls arrived.

From the records I have available to me, it appears that this is the period when things began to go terribly wrong for the family. Newspaper articles I have subsequently read identify the N.S.P.C.C. as having been involved with the family from 1959, onwards.

The story surrounding Karen Ann, the fourth child, born on 19th November 1959 is both tragic and suspicious. I will begin Karen's story with my own recollection of events and then the official reports and then leave you to draw your own conclusions.

At the time of Karen's birth, I would be almost five years old.

Photograph of Hillcrest Road Kates Hill. Taken 1960. Photographer Mr W H Massey, reproduced by Dudley Archives & Local History Service. These are the flats at Hillcrest Road, Kates Hill. We lived in the first block at the top (top left as you look at the picture). It appears the lamp post has the remnants of a rope swing, also, note the milk float parked outside the flats. I have no idea who the little girl is, but she would be around the same age as me, maybe she was someone we played games with?

TWO

Karen

RECORDS SHOW that Karen spent most her life in foster care, only being at home for around nine weeks, eight of those at the very beginning. It was no wonder then that my mother was unable to bond with her and accept her as her daughter.

My memory of her is of when she came home for a few days in November 1961, however, as records show she was returned to local authority care, thus missing her first birthday with us.

I remember her as being a woeful, sad child toddling about the flat, always crying and distressed. Now I look back at that time of her life I get the feeling that maybe Karen was unhappy being at the flat as this would have been a foreign place for her, maybe she was happier being with foster parents and more familiar surroundings.

I recall her as having thick black hair (a trait from her mother) and being quite a beautiful baby. According to records, she had spent nine months of the initial eleven months of her life at a home for very small children, returned home for a week, then being fostered out. She was then transferred to other foster parents in December 1960.

You will see from the newspaper records of the inquest that Karen died at home, at Hillcrest Road, what you will not see is the evidence from the inquest that Karen was indeed returned home for the final days of her life.

It is my belief that had Karen remained in care she would be alive today.

My memory of Karen's final days at home have tormented me all of my life, I have tried to believe that maybe what I witnessed was a dream from long ago, that the events of her final night really did not happen and maybe I mistakenly, with my tender years, got the events mixed up with someone else, somewhere else.

The more I try to dismiss the memory the more it is reinforced with the knowledge that this is what happened, I saw it and I will never forget it, it did happen and it happened to Karen.

I recall being in the flat, I can't remember if it was morning or evening. I do recall that my father was not at home. I can still see Karen crying and miserable with my mother at her wits end and shouting at her, making Karen even more distressed. At some point my mother picked her up and flung her across the room with some force, Karen landed in an armchair and stopped crying, she remained calm and quiet. I was too young and too naive to understand what was happening or the consequences.

That night as I lay in bed with Stephen, I remember waking up from a sleep and seeing a brilliant light emanating from my parents bedroom, I got out of bed to peek through the open door, leaving Stephen fast asleep. I can clearly remember seeing a white shining figure standing over Karen's cot, bending slightly over her as if to look at her, comfort her. I believe to this day that someone had called to take Karen away, I believe she was at that moment being released from the pain and torment that had befallen her small innocent life.

I went back to bed and slept.

The following morning of 28th April 1961, seventeen months after her birth, Karen was found dead in bed, discovered by my father. I remember him saying, "The baby's dead."

There are those who will say it was a dream I had that night, there are those who will say it was my imagination. But these are the memories of a child, who became a man and they are vivid memories which are significant and relative to that one single event.

From my research I have been able to identify that both Michael and Karen were buried in public graves with strangers, both without markings, a practice that was common when families were poor and unable to afford funeral costs. Michael was buried with two children aged two and five, buried in 1917 and 1941 respectively, neither were related to the family. Karen was buried with a 17 day old baby boy from 1940, his name was – **John Fisher** (no relation) when I was given that piece of information the hairs on the back of my neck stood up.

I found out by calling up the cemetery and giving the names, and dates of the deaths of both children, they were able to tell me the grave numbers. Whilst I have been to visit both, I would need assistance from the cemetery staff to identify the exact location.

To move on – the following are the exact copies of newspaper articles I came across many years ago during my research.

Express & Star   May 3rd 1961

Inquest on Dudley baby adjourned.

An inquest was opened at Dudley today on Karen Ann Fisher aged 17 months, of 102 Hillcrest Road Dudley, who was found dead in bed at home on the morning of April 28.

After taking evidence of identification from the father, Josiah Fisher, the coroner Mr Malcolm Wright, adjourned the inquiry to a date to be fixed.

Dudley Herald   May 5th 1961

Baby fractured her skull – but this was not the cause of death.

A 17 month old baby girl who fractured her skull when she fell downstairs was also suffering from acute bronchial pneumonia which caused her death, it was revealed at the Dudley inquest on Karen Ann Fisher of 102 Hillcrest Road Dudley.

"Death was due quite clearly to bronchial pneumonia," said Doctor H Baker, Pathologist. "The fractured skull and recent bleeding into the brain from small blood vessels played no part at all in the death." The Coroner Mr M Wright said he had held the inquest because of the history of the child's fall while in the care of the local authority and with foster parents.

"But in view of the evidence I do not think there is any need for me to comment about the way the child was treated. I am satisfied that the child did not die from the fractured skull, but from bronchial pneumonia and I shall therefore record a verdict of death from natural causes."

Two falls

The child went into the care of the local authority on January 7th 1960 and remained with them until October 29th at a home for very small children, said Mr Ronald Jones, Dudley Corporation Children's Officer.

She was returned to her home for a few days but as her mother was ill, she was returned to the care of the local authority on November 7th and was boarded out with foster parents and transferred to other foster parents on December 30th.

Mr Jones added, "I understand that on March 10th 1961 the foster mother was cleaning the bedroom and put Karen in one bedroom and closed the door firmly while she cleaned another."

While she was in this other bedroom the baby in some way opened the door and crawled to the top of the stairs and fell down them. After being treated for bruising she seemed to have recovered. A few days later she fell out of her pram onto a carpet and in view of her previous fall was taken to Dudley Guest Hospital and a fractured skull was diagnosed.

"It could not be decided which fall had caused the fracture," said Mr Jones.

The baby was discharged in a week as cured. Asked by the coroner if he could assure him that the foster parents looked after the child in a proper manner Mr Jones replied, "Yes, these parents have had short stay babies before on several occasions, we are quite satisfied with the way they looked after the children and we are quite satisfied that these falls were unfortunate accidents."

Well, that may be so, but I have a few questions to ask. Surely at 16 months Karen would have been walking, not **"crawling"** as the statement suggests? And if she was "crawling" how on earth did she manage to reach the door handle to open it? Also my recollection of Karen was of a child quite capable of walking at 17 months, not one that had only just learnt to stand up.

If a small child falls down a flight of stairs, I would expect the guardian to take them to the hospital, not wait until they fall out of a pram a few days later, and then take them. *"In view of the previous fall was taken to Dudley Guest Hospital"*, I would envisage the first fall to be slightly more serious? If they did take her to hospital following the first fall the report does not make this clear. Do we have to assume that had she not fallen out of her pram and the fractured skull was a result of the fall down stairs, this would have gone undetected?

Finally, I do understand that bronchial pneumonia can come on suddenly and is particularly dangerous to the very young, but why didn't someone close to the family or health visitors, who I know made regular visits, pick this up?

It appears to me that Karen was recovering from both these falls, but then she was allowed to go home. It was this decision in my opinion that spelled disaster for her. My mother was in no fit state to care for her, subsequent history of child care was to demonstrate this quite vividly. Both Stephen and I were older and able to cope, Karen was in the stranglehold of neglect.

My final memory of Karen was when I was sitting on the window sill of the flat one morning and seeing the hearse pulling up. It was to be nearly five decades before I would visit her again.

We spent around two years living at Hillcrest Road. It was here that I was to venture into my early experience of education, I recall my mother dragging me up the steep hill into primary school, kicking and screaming. Once there I seemed to settle down, at least for a short while.

Leading up to one Christmas, the first I can remember, my father bought Stephen and me bikes. He hid them in the bedroom, hopeful no doubt that we would not find them, we did. It was to be a bitterly cold Christmas that year, deep in snow, I recall my father taking us out into the street and teaching us how to ride. Many years later I was to discover from my grandmother Fisher that he had them on credit and never actually paid for them.

There were to be many occasions during the next three years when Stephen and I would be left in the flat to care for ourselves. One particular day I decided to make a pot of tea, I felt really proud of my achievement and that I had a pot of tea waiting for my father when he came home. Unfortunately I put a full quarter pound of tea into the pot, it must have tasted like tar when he tried it!

On a separate occasion Stephen and I sat in front of the television and proceeded to take it apart, we literally took every valve and wire out of it. I can't remember the consequences of our actions, but I would imagine it didn't go down well.

Early one evening, Stephen and I found ourselves standing outside the Castle Hill car park looking down at the circus that had arrived in town, Chipperfields as I recall. A young couple asked us if we wanted to go in, at that age I guess we were four and six, we were not going to say no. They took us in and bought us an ice cream each, we sat through the show and later went straight home. When I look back at that event I realise the danger we were not only putting ourselves in, but allowed to be put in through the neglect of our parents, and then I think what were this couple doing taking two young kids off the street into a circus for a couple of hours? I often wondered what their intentions must have been, were they philanthropic or were there other motives?

These episodes when we were left alone were due to my mother leaving the flat and doing whatever she needed to do, I assume my father was out working I remember him working some night shifts. I guess the fact that we were being left alone began to put enormous strain on my father and maybe this was the catalyst for the marital violence that ensued, or maybe it was where she was going and who with.

My first recollection of violence between my parents began at the flat. I can't remember the cause, I only remember my parents shouting at each other and my mother threw a steel milk crate at my father as he got to the bottom of the concrete steps that linked the ground and first floor, she was standing at the top at the time.

One particular night as it got dark, the violence once again erupted, my mother ran out of the flat down into the street and stood in the centre of the main road, screaming at traffic for someone to run her over and "end it".

My father's brother, my uncle Jim, came to the flat one evening and hit my father quite severely, I seem to recall he was angry at the way my father was behaving. I can't remember the exact argument or the cause, I do remember being quite upset and my mother comforting my father after my uncle left.

I then began to witness events which at the time meant very little to me. I was not at an age where I could understand what was happening, it was to be many years later before the realisation, pain and anger attached themselves to the memories.

On one occasion I was out with my mother, we went into a butcher's shop in Dudley, which incidentally no longer exists. My mother seemed to be getting on very well with the man behind the counter, she obviously made arrangements to see him later and when we got back home these three men arrived at the flat. I recall the first man going into the bedroom with my mother and coming out a little while later saying to his pal "your turn".

There was an occasion when my uncle (the husband of my mother's sister) came to the flat, I believe they had met in the town earlier that night. He tried every trick in the book to convince my mother to let him come inside the flat, however she was adamant she was not letting him in. I remember feeling all those years ago that this isn't right, he shouldn't be here treating my mother like this. I held an awful lot of contempt for this particular uncle for many years after. But I never discussed that night with anyone.

There were obviously things going on between my mother and father that I wasn't fully aware of. Around August 1960 both Stephen (aged two and nine months) and I (aged five and seven months) were received into the care of the local authority. We were placed with foster parents at Maple Road in Dudley. Records indicate the reason for reception into care was that my mother had left home her whereabouts unknown and my father reluctantly said he could not provide satisfactory care for us.

I have no memory of going to this address, however Social Service records indicate we were only there for a few days and then my father requested we were to be discharged to his care. One thing has always puzzled me, my father gave an address at Elmley Lovett near Hartlebury, presumably he was taking us there, I always planned to ask him why there? I never seemed to find the right opportunity to get round to it.

THREE

Social Services

RECORDS I have since recovered indicate that concern was expressed by the police and the N.S.P.C.C. for the welfare of the family. We never actually went to Hartlebury, we ended up back at Hillcrest Road, my father went to work and during the time he was out we were cared for by a neighbour living a few doors away.

My mother had been admitted to Barnsley Hall for treatment, this being a well known psychiatric hospital. The strange thing about all this is if we were under the supervision of Social Services and the N.S.P.C.C. why were we allowed to be cared for by a neighbour when our mother was in hospital and our father at work?

My mother must have returned home, but the situation once again deteriorated. In February 1961 my mother took me to Dudley Police Station, having left Stephen aged twenty-seven months alone in the flat and his position was reported to the police by neighbours. We were once again received into care, this time at a children's home called Saltwells. My mother spent the night at New Cross Hospital, a result of more marital violence I assume. According to records within a week we were back at home, the parents having become reconciled.

Over a period of time, my mother was being beaten by my father, the kids were in and out of care, a three year old was left on his own, my mother had been put into hospital and concern had already been expressed by both the police and the N.S.P.C.C. concerning the welfare of the family. Yet Social Services with all their wisdom allowed Karen aged sixteen months, to go home!

Karen went into care some seven months before Stephen and me, the reasons for this have never been made clear. Social Service records do not indicate the existence of Karen until her death in April 1961. Why was she placed into care at two months? If concern was raised at the inability of my mother to look after her children, why then was Stephen allowed to remain at home aged two, and myself for that matter?

At some point around about May 1962 the family were evicted from Hillcrest Road, I assume this was due to non payment of rent. It seems my father, Stephen and I went to live with my grandparents Fisher at Beech Green for what must have been a relatively short stay, before being taken into care. My mother, heavily pregnant, was living with her father at Bluebell Road. Stephen was placed into foster care with a family in Dudley, this family were unaware at the time of the vital role they would come to play in my life many years later.

I was placed into the care of foster parents also living in Dudley. I remember my time with this family rather well. The day I arrived I was taken there by a social worker, a Miss McShee. We arrived in a red car and the house stood back some distance from the road up a steep embankment. I recall being made welcome by the lady fostering me and later that evening when her husband arrived home I remember him telling me that if I behaved then we would all get on fine. There is one vivid memory that has stayed with me all of my life from this three month event, which is the multi-coloured blanket that adorned my bed, for some reason this has remained a focal point of my stay there.

My foster mother was a wonderful person and did her best to make me feel welcome. She had two children of her own, a boy (Peter) older than me and a daughter (Christine) about my age. It must be difficult for natural children to accept a strange child into their home, they must feel a kind of invasion and demands placed upon their parents, parents they felt were exclusive to them.

My first day was difficult, attempting to adjust to my new surroundings. During the short time, about three months or so I spent with this family I became withdrawn and unhappy. I felt quite alone, I sensed the other two children began to resent my presence, especially the older son. These two were used to playing together and they made it quite clear that they did not want anyone else around their home.

I recall one day I helped them both create a kind of 'camp' in the garden, I felt really excited about being involved at last and we seemed to be hitting it off.

However, when the camp was finished I was not allowed to play in it and that moment brought home to me how unwelcome I really was.

As the days passed the nights became unbearable, at least during the day I had things to occupy my mind, at night I would cry myself to sleep. I remember staring through the bedroom window into a totally foreign world, not knowing where I was or how far away was home.

My thoughts turned to running away, but where would I run to? How long I wondered would I have to endure living here. Would I see my mother, father and brother again? The summer nights were long and darkness didn't come quickly, giving me more time to reflect.

My thoughts often turned to my Aunt Alice (my mother's sister) who we had visited quite often, I felt very close to her and I became confused as to why I couldn't stay with her rather than strangers.

Eventually the time came for me to leave. I remember one day I caught sight of my foster mother crying on the shoulder of her husband, saying she couldn't cope any longer. I perceived this had something to do with me and a few days later I was returned to the children's home at Saltwells. I recall my mother visiting me at Saltwells, we sat out on the steps and she tried to comfort me by saying we would be back together soon, it was really difficult for me to say goodbye to her.

During my stay with foster parents my mother had given birth on the 27th May 1962 to her fifth child, a boy she named Thomas William, it was to be some time before I saw Thomas. Social Service reports from this time indicate that my mother was homeless and had left my father. She had been temporarily accommodated at 'Lawnswood House' an old peoples' home.

My first sight of Thomas was during a visit to the zoo, which my father had arranged for us but even this ended in arguments and upsets. After coming away from the zoo my father had to return me to the children's home and my mother, who was staying at the old peoples' home following the birth of Thomas, refused to return there. She had the baby in his pram and wanted to go to her father's house in Bluebell Road. My father said this was unwise and didn't want her to go there. After some arguing my father decided to put me into a taxi and send me back to the children's home and he eventually gave in to my mother and took her to her father's house, my granddad Nicklin. During that evening she turned up at my grandparents' house at Beech Green where my father was staying. My father allowed her to stay the night and took her back the next day.

It appears my grandparents were away on holiday at this point, I have no doubt that had they been at home my mother would not have been allowed to stay.

Once again in September 1962 my parents were reconciled and living at 25 Pitman Street, Kate's Hill in Dudley. It appears this is where they had been moved to in June, following the eviction from Hillcrest Road. We were discharged from care and allowed to go back to them and the next twelve months were to be the most traumatic in my life, and the last time we would be together as a family.

Pitman Street was without any shadow of a doubt a slum. One side of the street was full of empty houses, vacated many years before. The fact that we had been evicted from the flat and placed here, was I think a last resort on behalf of the council and Social Services to house us and keep the family together.

The house was a two bedroom property. All the houses were joined together, about thirty each side, running top to bottom of the street. At the rear they were separated into blocks of four. Our block had an entrance at the rear, which came in really handy at times, especially if the truancy officer called, we could scarper out the back.

There were other neighbours living in the street, but not many. I remember the next door neighbours were a couple who I believe were middle-aged with no children. I can't imagine what they must have thought of us lot moving in. A little way further up the street was a neighbour I often spoke to. A tall blonde middle-aged woman, who seemed to take an interest in us, possibly out of concern for the conditions we were living in.

The front door was old and worn and let in all the cold and draughts. The windows were tiny and made of metal which over the years had rusted and decayed due to neglect. The panes of glass were thin and some with cracks and holes in them. The front room was small, on one wall two or three steps leading to a wooden pantry door up to the bedrooms, on another adjacent wall, the opening to the kitchen.

There was an open coal fire in the front room, but due to the cost of coal and coke it was barely lit. No electricity existed in the house, light was obtained by means of lighting gas mantles situated on the walls. These worked by a means of a small mantle that had to be regularly replaced, they were constructed of a very flimsy material. I lost count of the times I attempted to light these delicate mantles, only to catch them with my hand and see them disintegrate.

We had no television in the house whilst we were there. My mother had no washing machine, no electricity you see! The only form of entertainment came by means of a radio, which I assume was battery powered.

The house was cold and damp, a miserable place to live. My mother, father and Thomas shared one bedroom, Stephen and I the other, even these didn't have doors. Outside was a toilet and washing area that had long ago been abandoned for washing purposes. The toilet was designed to be used by all four terraced houses, however only ourselves and the couple next door remained to use this facility.

The washing area was a throwback to Victorian times, a shared wash-house for the four houses where the woman of the house could do all her washing, placing the clothes in a cylindrical basin, wash them through then use a 'mangle' to squeeze out any excess water. The laundry was fed between two rollers, usually made of wood but sometimes covered with rubber and turned by a handle at the side, before placing them on a washing line.

Soap was used in the days before detergents. White laundry went in first as it needed the hottest water, this was removed with tongs and darker items followed. The washboard was used for delicate items, a 'dolly' for other laundry. Some items required boiling, taking anything from half an hour to half a day! There was a flat board placed over the basin when not in use.

At the time we moved in I would be seven years of age, Stephen was five and Thomas about four months. I remember Thomas being a happy baby, smiling and fairly content.

However, the one thing that has puzzled me for some time is that when I reflect on the fact that Karen was removed to care after two months of her life and the circumstances surrounding the family history during the period leading up to and following her death, why was Thomas, another new baby, placed in the care of my parents?

Our house when we eventually moved in would be on the bottom right, about four houses up. You can see the derelict yard about half way up the street on the left where Stephen and I had many adventures.

Stephen should at this time have been going to school, I can't remember being at school with him, but then the time we were at Pitman Street I hardly ever went to school myself. I remember the school I frequented occasionally and I remember that none of the kids there would have anything to do with me, due to the fact that I smelt to high heaven and was covered in head lice. I don't recall there being soap in the house, I can't say we ever really washed. Our clothes were thrown in a pile up the corner of the kitchen, along with the soiled nappies from Thomas. We simply rummaged through the pile of clothing and put on whatever we came across. My shoes had holes in them and had come apart from the soles and would 'flap' up and down as I walked.

My memories of Pitman Street are happy memories, when I think back to the things we did and the freedom we were allowed, due in the main I must admit to neglect, that is to say my father was very rarely at home to see what was going on, and my mother didn't really care. Maybe I'm being a little unkind, I think it was the fact that she didn't appreciate her duties as a mother. Later on it was to be revealed that the authorities didn't regard the neglect as 'wilful neglect'.

So what was life really like for us, myself aged seven, Stephen five and Thomas four months, at Pitman Street? Well you will recall that there were

Photograph of Pitman Street taken around 1959, Photographer-Mr W H Massey.
Picture reproduced courtesy of Dudley Archives & Local History Service.

incidents of domestic violence at Hillcrest Road? These continued at Pitman Street, I never really worked out what caused these arguments and fights I just remember that all of a sudden it would 'kick off'.

One night my father came home and asked my mother where his tea was, she I recall was at the sink. She made some sort of comment and turned around and hit him with a milk bottle. I realised what was going to happen and got Stephen and Thomas out of the house, we stood outside by the door, listening to the mayhem going on inside. As the fighting continued the windows were broken and I could hear furniture breaking. When things quietened down I went back inside and I will never forget the scene before me, every piece of furniture we had, and there wasn't a lot, had been destroyed almost as if someone had taken an axe to it.

The effects of having to listen to my parents hitting each other, the verbal abuse and the cuts and bruises I saw have stayed with me all of my life. Even today I can tolerate two men fighting or two women, but whenever I witness a man and women fighting, I have visions of my childhood days, the memories come flooding back and I have to distance myself.

It wasn't always like that at home, there were times when we were happy. Stephen and I got up to all sorts of escapades. One day Stephen and I went into one of the derelict houses opposite, it was a decaying property with wallpaper hanging from the walls, smelling of damp and rot. We found our way to the wash house I described earlier and we climbed up onto the board covering the basin and got hold of a piece of string. Above the basin was a kind of beam which I presume was for hanging the washing on when it came out of the tub. I tied the piece of string to the beam and made a noose from the other end. At some point Stephen tried to jump off the basin onto the floor but got caught up in the noose around his neck, the board gave way underneath him and he hung precariously swinging with the noose around his neck, going blue in the face.

I realised there was little I could do, or maybe I just simply panicked, anyway, fortunately at that time my mother was at home. I ran across the street to tell her what had happened. She ran across to rescue him and pull him down. Had she not been at home that day, which would not have been uncommon, I feel certain Stephen would not be here today. He had a bright red mark around his neck for some days later.

Adjacent to the house there was a disused yard. One day we decided to climb over and investigate. We came across a number of boxes, being inquisitive we decided to remove one or two and take a look inside. Having got them open we discovered they contained hundreds of bullets, bright brass coloured shells. I can't imagine how they got there or why they were not made secure.

Anyway, being totally naive we took them to an area away from the house and began to hit the ends of them with bricks, obviously to see if they were live, or in our minds, if we could get them to 'go off'. Someone must have seen us in the yard nicking this stuff, as a few minutes went by and the police arrived. They questioned us as to where we got these bullets from and removed them. I never did discover if they were 'live' or not, I guess had the police not arrived when they did we might have found out! So it seems on reflection that not being successful in attempting to 'hang' Stephen, I later tried to 'shoot' him.

One day Stephen and I went walkabouts, I can't remember where we ended up, but I recall eating what we thought were 'peas' from a tree. It was some kind of weeping willow, or 'wattle tree' with these pods hanging from it. By the time we got back home we both felt very sick with a terrible stomach pain. My mother had been out and brought us a chocolate, I believe that was the only time we refused sweets.

FOUR

Little Thieves

I MENTIONED earlier my time at primary school was not a happy one. Between the ages of five and eight I must have been to most primary schools in the area, moving between foster parents and children's homes, every time going to a different school. During my time at Pitman Street I went to Kate's Hill School.

Due to the family circumstance we received free school dinners, this was really the only meal I had during the day, the only other stuff available to us at home was bread with sauce or dripping. I realised that whilst we were being fed at school there was little for Thomas back home so I devised a cunning caper.

I would have my dinner at school, but when I went up for my pudding I would never have custard on it, this allowed me to put the pudding in my pocket and take it home for Thomas. Anything was better than nothing.

I spent a fair amount of my time looking after baby Thomas, changing his nappy for something a bit more decent, usually a small rag of something I found amongst the pile of filth in the kitchen, though I do believe he suffered with nappy rash quite a bit.

Our time at the house during the evenings when my mother was in was spent listening to the radio. I still remember dressing up in any clothes we could find and singing and dancing to the tunes of *Sing Something Simple* a half-hour radio programme which featured Cliff Adams and The Cliff Adams Singers, with Jack Emblow on accordion. The programme ran for 42 years from 1959 until 2001, whenever I hear that signature tune I remember those nights and the way my mother used to laugh at us, and the laughter and screams that came from Thomas, watching us dancing around the room.

But it wasn't all laughter.

One day, having no food in the house and no money to buy any, my mother asked Stephen and I to go into town and to 'George Masons', a small supermarket, some of you will no doubt remember. However, we had no money, as I said, and our mother made it clear that we were to get what we could and walk out, in effect we were being sent to 'shoplift'.

I still remember quite clearly as if it were yesterday, walking around the shop placing items in a bag, the strange thing was we had a dog at the time and most of the stuff in the bag was dog food. As we attempted to walk out the shop we were stopped by the manager who asked me for the receipt. I recall saying I had thrown it down, and I "have definitely paid for this lot". He didn't swallow it for a minute and carted us back into the back room ready to phone the police.

The woman I mentioned earlier, living a few doors away from us, worked on the tills and asked the manager to let us go, saying "they're just babies". But no! He said it was the principle of the thing and was nicking us.

I recall being carted up the stairs at Dudley Police Station and sitting in a room waiting to be interviewed, wondering what was going to happen to us. Some time later we were taken home. I remember my father hitting the roof because of what we had done and proceeded to take it out on my mother. For that little escapade I received three years probation, Stephen got off scot free, I think!

My probation officer was the great Mr Bert Bissell. Born in Dudley, Worcestershire, in January 1902, he founded the Young Men's Bible Class at Vicar Street Methodist Church in the town in 1925. He led a pilgrimage party from the Bible Class to the summit of Ben Nevis on VJ Day in 1945 and constructed a 'Peace Cairn', he died in November 1998, aged 96. My Dad used to take me to see him occasionally as part of my probation terms.

The dog never did get his freebie! And some time later in a fit of temper my mother hit him over the head with a full milk bottle, killed him and threw him in the pantry. Stephen was screaming because of what she'd done, so she threw Stephen in with the dog.

One day whilst at home a knock came at the door, my mother answered and standing there was a short fellow well dressed, selling insurance or something of that kind. Being inquisitive, as kids are, we stood at the side of mother listening intently. The conversation got round to him wanting to come in, but the 'kids' were home. So he offered us sixpence (about two and a half pence), which was quite a lot back in 1963. He asked us to go to the shops to spend it and take our time. Not being one to turn down a good offer when I saw it, we promptly set off. I can't remember how long we were away, but when we got back he'd gone. It wasn't until many years later and subsequent other events that happened that I realised what went on that day.

It would be easy for me to make judgements concerning my mother's behaviour both back at Hillcrest Road and Pitman Street. However, when I look back at how we were living our lives and the struggle she had trying to bring us up and feed us with no money coming in, I realise that on occasions she had to do things to put food on the table.

You might well ask where my father was at this time and why he was not providing for us. Let me share an extract from a newspaper report I came across!

Dudley Herald   Sat July 27th 1963

Man Blamed For Wife's offence
The father of three children was blamed for his wife's appearance before Dudley magistrates on Monday.

Alderman A.M. Silcox told the husband, "You are the one who is to blame because you have not looked after her." Mrs Margaret Magdalene Fisher (27) of 25 Pitman Street, Dudley admitted stealing a pension book and trying to get her eight year old son to cash a forged order for £2.17s.6p at a post office.

The husband Josiah Fisher elected to give evidence on his wife's behalf and said he was unable to work because his wife was an epileptic and he had to stay at home to look after the children.

Alderman Silcox told him, "If you had not given evidence we should have called you, for we think from the report we have, that you are responsible for your wife being here, by not giving her the support you should. The impression we have is that it is you who should be here, and if it was we should send you to prison."

Chief Inspector L. Stafford said the pension book was delivered by a postman to Mrs Fisher's home, the pensioner having lived there previously. She sent her son to the post office but the sub postmaster did not pay out any money and told the police.

Mrs Fisher told W.P.C A. Ross that her husband had been unemployed for sometime and she got £6.00 a week from him and 18s family allowance.

There were children aged eight, five and one year. She told the court that when she tried to get the money she had not a penny in her purse and there was no food in the house.

Alderman Silcox said to Mrs Fisher, "we hope that after this your husband will turn over a fresh leaf with regard to looking after you, we are not holding you to blame for this, because your husband should have taken care of you."

The chairman said that Mrs Fisher would be put on probation for two years. "We shall remit the costs of 30s, because we don't want to give you any more financial trouble than you already have." He remarked.

Well it is fairly obvious that things didn't improve, some time later my mother having no money in the house broke into the gas meter and stole the money from it. When this was discovered my father accepted the blame for it, in order to keep her out of further trouble, and was subsequently fined. He failed to pay the fine and was sentenced to four months in prison. So there we were no father at home, no money coming in, a mother and three children left to the mercy of the outside world.

My mother had no real control over what Stephen and I were up to. The one night we were playing a few yards from the house, it was quite dark and we were throwing stones at each other when one stone hit a car windscreen and broke it. We ran back to the house and a few minutes later came a knock on the door, it was the guy who owned the car obviously coming to sort us out.

My mom opened the door to him with Stephen and me cowering behind her. He took one look inside the house another look at us and said something to the effect, "These two just broke my car window but never mind." Then just walked away. I think he realised there was absolutely no point in asking us to pay for the damage.

In order to understand what was happening to us and perhaps why, let me explain. My mother may or may not have been mentally ill, she was a woman with 'limited intelligence' so the psychologists said. She just did not understand that she had responsibilities, part of which was to care for her children.

She did things that other responsible mothers would never do, she had no concept of the dangers she was putting us in. She would go out and leave the three of us alone in the house. She did this many, many times even when we were younger and living at Hillcrest Road. She simply didn't understand that we were in danger. One report I came across stated that the children were in 'moral' danger. We were not being taught the real values of life, or how to behave correctly.

There was no stability in our lives and no real role models to give us guidance. We basically did what we wanted, when we wanted, if we chose not to go to school then we didn't. If we chose to stay out till late, very late, then we did, we came home when we got tired.

There were times when our mother would go out in the early evening, and she always made sure she looked her best. I remember her as being a tall woman around six feet in height. She was very beautiful, I know this from memory and from the only photograph I have of her when she was about seventeen.

She always wore bright red lipstick. This is something I have come to detest on other women, I really have a problem with any women that wear bright red lipstick. I think it comes from seeing my mother wear it and the incidents surrounding her life, it's almost as if I have developed a conscious picture of her wearing it and associating it with the things she did. It in effect reminds me of her and draws me back to the days I am about to discuss.

I'm not certain if she went out every night, I suspect she didn't, probably Friday nights and weekends, but I may be wrong. I know that on occasions she would go into town and pawn her wedding ring in order to obtain some money, I often went with her to the pawnbrokers.

When things began to go wrong, I mean terribly wrong and my father was no longer around, there was little, if any money coming in. Social Services back then did what they could, money was available from a social fund called 'National Assistance' (the briars) however, I am not aware there was money available to support families as there is today.

FIVE

Getting Worse

I NEVER had any real concept at such a tender age of how families lived, how they paid bills or paid for food, I just accepted that it was there. As children we don't think of things like that, it's not our responsibility, we rely on our parents to provide for us and get on with the business of being children.

My mother however, had to provide for us in the best way she could, she had to generate some income, she couldn't go out to work and no one in the family was prepared to help support her. So she turned to the only thing she could, she used herself to bring money in. It wouldn't be the first time she had to resort to prostitution. There was the time at Hillcrest Road with the three men from the butcher's and the salesman at Pitman Street. It was not for self gratification, but out of sheer necessity.

She frequented a number of public houses in the town centre, many of them still stand today. Two however are now occupied by other premises.

I recall she had a friend called Alma who lived opposite the flat in Hillcrest Road. Alma would very often visit my mum and was aware of how my father was treating her, hitting her etc. I think Alma lived alone but was well known in the area and I suspect had already been well initiated into prostitution. I believe her influence encouraged my mother to embark on this path.

Stephen and I would spend many nights sitting on a step opposite one particular pub, we would be there in the rain and the cold while my mother was inside having a good time, having her drinks paid for and then going round the back of the pub with whoever had the money to pay for her.

One particular night, having waited for what seemed an eternity, feeling cold and miserable, I went into the pub to find my mother, to encourage her to come home. I wandered through the lounge and snug, searching for her. I found her out the back with a black guy. I walked away and continued to wait a little longer, on the step, in the cold huddled together to keep warm, oblivious to what was going on.

You're probably thinking 'where was Thomas in all of this?' He was with me, I never left him on his own, if my mother went out and left us and I decided to go and find her, then we all went together, however, there came a point when we could no longer do this. The pram my mother received from Social Services to transport the baby around in became another target for Stephen and me. We removed the wheels and made a 'trolley' out of it. I clearly recall belting down the hill as fast has we could in the middle of the road.

And why, whilst all this was going on, didn't someone report it? How could people ignore three small children sitting on a step late at night in the middle of the town centre? Well, not all of them did, some would ask if we were ok, some would ask what we were doing. I would tell them the truth, "it's ok, we're waiting for our mom, she'll be out in a minute." Then they'd simply walk away.

We arrived at a point in our lives where we were destitute! We were not going to school and when the school inspector arrived at the house one day and I knew who he was, because he'd been before, we would hide. Mother knew of course we were there, but denied any knowledge of the fact, saying she had sent us to school, therefore she didn't know where we were.

We ran wild, doing whatever we wanted. The fact that I hadn't been to school much and had been moved around in care so many times in the last three years, meant I couldn't read or write at the age of eight. We never washed and wore the same clothes day after day. It was only a matter of time before the system caught up with us, this couldn't go on, something had to happen and it did, big time!

That day was in September 1963. I didn't realise it then of course, but it was to be the last day we would be together as a family, Thomas was going to disappear from my life and the next time I would see my little brother would be twenty two years later!

At this point my father was serving a prison sentence for non payment of a fine, you remember the gas meter incident? He must have been doing some sort of work before he went to prison, because I remember my mother saying she and I were going out that morning and we were going to collect his wages from a job he'd been doing. We left the house early that morning, just her and me, we left Thomas and Stephen behind in the house. The open fire was left blazing, Thomas would be 17 months old and Stephen six years at this time.

I remember going down to Great Bridge, but that's about all I recall. Later on we arrived at Dudley market and my mother bought me a couple of items, one I vividly remember being some sort of bracelet, brightly coloured, I have no idea what became of it. Later on towards teatime, I guess, we arrived back home.

There to greet us were the Police and Social Services, it appears that a neighbour fearing for the welfare of Stephen and Thomas had called the police. I can't remember what was said but I know that Stephen and Thomas were not there, it seems they had been removed from the house earlier and taken into care. The authorities had to wait for my mother and me to return.

I was taken into Rydal children's home where my two brothers had already been taken. A report I came across confirmed these actions, the time the authorities arrived at the house, and found the two children alone: "Considering the conditions of the home the children were removed to the Police station, a doctor was sent for, photographs of the children were taken and they were then removed to a children's home."

I wasn't aware of it at the time, but I was never going back to Pitman Street and would never be together with my father and mother again. At this point in my life the family ceased to exist as a unit.

A little while later proceedings were taken and we arrived in court. A report from the day stressed that the proceedings were brought in order to prevent cruelty to the children. Mr **** asked for their removal from the care of these "ineffectual parents". The mother was now undergoing medical treatment for epilepsy, and the father was serving a prison sentence for non payment of a fine. Inspector ****** of the N.S.P.C.C. said that he had been trying to help the family from 1959 onwards: "It has come to the point that whenever the mom goes out, the Police or I have had to care for the kids" and, "on one occasion the baby had been left alone in the house for almost 3 hours." He had given the mother a pram so that she could take the baby with her when she went out, but within three weeks the pram was useless (what he didn't say was that Stephen and I had taken the bloody wheels off, and made a wooden go cart from it).

The report went on to say subsequently an older boy aged eight was admitted to the home on a voluntary basis with his mother's consent, the inspector asked if she had any objections to the children staying in the home until October 8th, the mother replied, "I don't want them to be there that long, I want them to be with me, I can't live on my own." She added, "I have got clothes for them, I have bought them everything."

Mr A A ******* chairman of the magistrates said the interim order would be made and the mother cried, "Why should they stay there? I suppose when he comes home he will take it out on me." Inspector ****** explained she was referring to her husband who was not in court and said that arrangements were being made for him to attend court on October 8th.

The mother then pleaded, "Why can't my sister have him?" As she was being led from the court she tried to approach the baby who was sitting on the knee of a man from the children's home. "I want to talk to him," said the mother, "leave me alone."

Her two boys began to cry and were comforted by a woman from the children's home. As the mother's protests became louder she was removed with difficulty from the court, as she was being led out she kicked a Police woman who had asked her to "quieten down", in her temper and confusion she blamed the Police woman for the events in court and lashed out at her. This incident led to her presentation back in court a week later, what happened there I can't say!

We were taken back to the children's home. My father was in prison at this time and read a newspaper article concerning the three children being taken into care. He told his mate in his cell "these are my kids".

I remember the children's home very well. In fact there were two homes I went into, one as stated was Rydal and the other was Saltwells. Saltwells was set within a large nature reserve, surrounded by thick dense forestry. It was a large house catering for a number of children, I have a vivid memory of driving through the forest for what seemed an eternity, stopping to open a metal swing gate, and closing it behind us, before arriving at the front of the house.

I spent a lot of hours playing under a large conifer tree that seemed to extend to the heavens, such was its height. The only friend I recall here was a lad named Joseph Probatt, I never found out what happened to Joseph.

I would spend a lot of time walking through the rear of the forest which continued for some length before opening onto residential land. On one occasion I had climbed some distance up a tree only to be poked with a large stick by one of the other kids and subsequently fell to the ground.

I can only remember my mother visiting me on one occasion, we sat talking on the steps looking out into the thick forest, I can't remember the conversation, but I recall the tears I shed when the time came for her to leave. No one ever came to visit at Rydal.

Apart from the two children's homes I also went to two foster carers, one I have already described, but more about that later. I guess I must have been in and out of care for a few years, off and on. It seems Social Services had control of my life for something like thirteen years.

In 2007 I went back to Saltwells, just to look at it and take a few photographs of the outside. I could still hear amongst the silence of the forest, the children inside the building, footsteps across the wooden floors, running around, up and down the stairs laughing. Children being children.

Anyway about Rydal, Rydal unlike Saltwells was set in a residential area of Dudley. There were only a handful of children residing at the house during my time there. I recall one particular stay there when I arrived bedraggled and dirty,

Saltwells children's home showing the doorstep where I sat with my mother.
The home is now closed and derelict.

The massive conifer tree where I spent many hours playing.

I was taken upstairs, stripped unceremoniously and given a bath by one of the female workers, trying where I could to hide my embarrassment.

I still have flashbacks of my time at Rydal when I smell the newness of clothes, memories of the time I was handed new pyjamas at the home. They seemed to have a stash of new clothing for new arrivals all neatly separated and in age order, trousers, shirts, underwear socks etc.

A few days into my stay I was asked what school I attended. I hadn't been to school for some time, so had no idea of the name or location, so I used my imagination and knew of a school in the town centre and off the top of my head said "the school by the bus terminus". So the next morning having breakfasted, I got into the car belonging to one of the care workers and proceeded to be dropped off at this totally foreign school. I got out of the car with some trepidation, wondering should I cough up or just play along. Well I decided to play along.

I walked the short distance into the school playground and disappeared behind the wall. I waited there some time allowing for the worker to disappear and promptly walked straight back out. I knew I had to go somewhere, but where? Well, my Aunt Alice sprang to mind, I thought, 'Yes! That's where I'll head for'. Conjuring a tale of "They let me out for the day to come and visit you".

I made my way to my aunt's and spent most of the day there, wondering to myself where will I go later? I had no intention of returning to the home, afraid more than anything of the repercussions of my lies and actions. I figured out I would spend the night over the nearby fields and then see what tomorrow brought.

Fortunately for my own safety, this never became an option I had to act out. My aunt realising quite astutely I had lied through my back teeth, took me to the local shop with her to get some groceries for my uncle's tea. Unbeknown to me and due to the fact she had no telephone in the house, asked the shopkeeper to call the police and explain what I had done. Looking back, this action must have been quite upsetting for her.

Later that afternoon, the police arrived at her address with a couple of social workers to take me back to the children's home. I recall crying and kicking out at the adults trying to get me in the car. I wanted to stay with my aunt, with someone I knew, not more strangers.

I was taken back to the home and I sobbed uncontrollably for some time, standing by the side door of the home looking out, not wanting any contact with anyone. One of the care workers came out to talk to me, I remember saying, "Don't worry, I won't run off again, no one wants me, I have no where to go now."

At that moment in my life I felt the whole world was against me. I went back inside and ate the three sausages they had prepared me for my tea. My parents were somewhere, where? I had no idea. I felt my aunt had deserted me and I felt quite alone. My brothers had disappeared and I really feared I would never see my family again.

The following day I returned to the school I had previously absconded from St Joseph's Primary in Dudley. I went to a variety of schools in Dudley, Sledmere Primary, Wrens Nest Primary, The Priory Primary, Kate's Hill Primary and St John's Primary. I found it difficult to learn, always playing 'catch up'. I started to learn to read and write then went to another school where the kids were in front of me, I found myself behind the rest of the class. I recall starting to learn decimals, then going to the next school and finding the class I was in had already done them. I was completely lost, on occasions I just had to sit there.

However, St Joseph's was to be the start of my long term education. I continued to attend the school and stayed there until the age of eleven, during which time I was educated primarily by the Nuns. One in particular became my favourite, though not a teacher, but head of the school Sister Lucy, she seemed to take a special interest in me, perhaps because of my background.

I settled down and began to learn to read and write, to get to grips with decimals and the rest of the curriculum and pass the first part of the 'Eleven Plus', to the amazement of all concerned. I didn't quite make the second part, but then time was against me. I had just one afternoon off during those three years.

The reason for this early and initial settlement came about through my aunt and uncle deciding they would have me to stay with them. It seems my aunt was so concerned about the way I got upset, having to be dragged away and the thought of me staying in care that they decided to care for me.

I was once asked by a dear friend, "What single event changed your life? What was the impetus? Was there a single individual?" On reflection I say, "Yes there was." My aunt Alice!

She could have let me go that day and forgotten me, instead she and my uncle Jack decided to take me in, to care for me, not for extra income as a foster child but because she loved me. She saw in me a need to be loved, a need to be wanted. She saw to my education, she bathed me, clothed me and gave me food, nourishment and love. And when I did anything wrong which on occasions I did, she corrected me. She instilled in me the values and morals I have today. She put into place the building blocks that transformed me from the ragged wretch of the boy I once was, to the man I am today. She my mother's sister!

On occasions I visit her final resting place and I weep.

I stayed with my aunt Alice and uncle Jack for about three years, during which time I experienced three birthdays and Christmas's. That might sound a strange statement to make, however, I had never experienced a birthday or a Christmas in the way other children experience them. We didn't get cards and we didn't get presents.

Christmas was a time for children, but when you had no money coming in you had no celebrations, no presents and a pretty miserable time. One Christmas whilst at Pitman Street we had a visit from the Social Worker who brought us a box of toys of other families hand me downs. I recall a big plastic red train singled out by me to play with, that is my only good memory of Christmas.

Whilst at my aunt's I had a Scalextric for one Christmas, a Timex wrist watch for the second, when I learnt to tell the time and a bike for the third.

I recall my first encounter with the opposite sex at Rosewood Road. I became quite fond of a little girl called Susan, who I guess became my girlfriend whilst I was there, well in the eyes of an eight year old that is. For one dreadful moment during one summer day I nearly ruined everything! We had built a small unassuming 'camp' over the fields which lay about thirty yards from the houses. Dug out into the ground and covered with planks of wood, old carpet etc. The both of us found ourselves sitting in this 'camp' and I asked her,

"Do you know how babies are made?"

To which she replied, "No!"

"Would you like to find out?" I said. At which point her mother called out to her to return home. I still wonder to this day what would have happened if her mother had not intervened at that precise moment in time? When I think about it I have visions of being locked up, ridiculed and traumatised for the rest of my life. Not because I could have actually done anything to her, that just wasn't possible, but the thought of trying to.

It seems obvious that with my upbringing and the things I had seen, my values and without doubt my morals had not been instilled in me at this point. Though I nearly instilled something in her!

Moving on! Due to the fact my aunt was my mother's sister, my mother would visit the house. The other issue that compounded the problem was the close proximity of my mother's brother and her father, my uncle Ted and my grandfather living right next door. It seemed whenever my mother visited she would find a way of upsetting me, how I can't recall, but I have flashbacks of tears whenever she was there. I know my uncle Jack didn't like the idea of her visiting, but as my aunt would say "she is his mother". My father lived with his parents during this time, my mother had been offered a council house not a million miles from where I was, about one in fact.

I became quite attached to my uncle Ted living next door, I guess I adopted him as a father figure, a role model if you like. I would spend lots of time round the house with both him and my grandfather, talking about the "olden days" and in particular the war years.

I never really played outside with other kids, apart from Susan, or went anywhere other than the occasional visits to North Wales to visit my uncle Jack's mother 'Mrs Pete' as we called her. Although I settled into this new home and way of living I often asked my aunt, "What has happened to Thomas?"

I knew Stephen had gone to live with my father's sister Joan and I believed he was okay, though I only saw him perhaps once a year. "Thomas," I was told, "I don't know where he is, someone must have him, but I don't know who." I could never come to terms with that, not a single person I spoke to, my mother, my father, aunts, uncles, no one knew where Thomas was.

I continued to live my life best as I could, going to school and playing just outside the front gate, occasionally venturing over the fields, but never really going too far. My aunt would stay at home, she never worked, due in part I think to the severe arthritis she suffered in her hands, they were quite distorted, badly twisted and I know she suffered with them, particularly during cold spells.

My uncle Jack worked for Tarmac, the road builders. Every time he returned home you could smell the 'tar' on him. My aunt and uncle had a German

Shepherd dog named 'Tassy', she was really my uncle's dog, he absolutely loved her and she him. Each night at around 4.50pm, she would stand up against the fence he had built to keep her in, looking for him to come walking down the street, her tail would start to wag and there he was, coming round the corner. I swear that dog had a sixth sense.

During the three years I stayed with my aunt Alice I never really had many exciting adventures. By the way I forgot to mention that her son 'Ted' who was much older than me also lived with us. This is him (far right) my uncle Ted (my mother's sister) next to him.

Ted was Alice's son, but not my uncle Jack's. Apparently my aunt was seeing a fellow many years before she met uncle Jack and got pregnant by him, he wanted nothing to do with her after that and left the scene. My uncle Jack met my aunt and married her taking Ted as his own son, they never had children of their own.

I didn't really have many friends apart from Susan and two brothers living opposite, they became the bane of my life at one point. I suffered from boils, abscesses appearing on different parts of my body, particularly nasty when you have one in the fold of your arm or the back of the neck. My aunt preferred the old fashioned method of treatment, to lance them with a hot bread poultice. She would soak bread in boiling water sandwiched between two lint clothes then 'slap' it on the boil. I can tell you I used to dread the times she would say "you need a poultice on that". The two lads I mentioned living opposite would take great delight in smacking me on the back of the neck in the vicinity of the boil.

It seems the reason I suffered this particular affliction of continual boils, was due to the fact I was run down. No, I wasn't hit by a bus. I was suffering from bad nerves, a condition identified by my GP following a visit to the Barber's no less. He noticed a bald patch on the back of my neck and suggested to my aunt I should "get it seen to". At this point in my life I was suffering a nervous breakdown, I remember having to take tablets for quite a while.

SIX

The Move

HAVING SETTLED at my aunt's and getting used to a fairly normal life was not to last, but then, this was becoming a familiar pattern for me.

I only ever remember my father visiting me once at my aunt and uncle's. On that occasion he hit my uncle Jack because he would not allow him into the house. The argument surrounded my uncle's belief that one visit in three years was simply unacceptable.

Subsequent investigations later on in my life and discussions with my father seemed to indicate that my father believed my mother was visiting her father living next door and popping round to see me at my aunt's. He believed my mother was still having an influence in my life and wanted to sever this connection between us. He eventually managed to do this by having me removed from my aunt and uncle's care into his care at my grandmother's (his mother).

At this point I would be eleven years of age. The separation came in the summer holidays of 1966. Having left primary school I was getting used to the thought of beginning my first term at the local comprehensive at Wren's Nest, however, I never got there.

I can't recall how my aunt broke the news to me that I would be moving out, or when. The day arrived for me to go with my uncle Jack to the Magistrate's Court at Dudley, then situated in Priory Street, before it was moved to the now present site at the Inhedge. I found out many weeks later that my aunt Alice could not face coming with us, my uncle and I, because I guess she realised he would be coming home without me.

I sat in the waiting room of the courts whilst my uncle and father debated the various reasons as to who should now have custody of me. My father came and sat by me for a while and said "this is for the best". He explained how my grandmother would look after me from now on, that he would be with me and I could have the things I wanted. He asked me if there was anything I really wanted, I couldn't think of anything at that time.

I was once again confused and bewildered at what was happening to me, why again was I being uprooted when I felt perfectly happy where I was?

Then came a moment in my life I will never forget. I was taken into the court room, asked to stand in front of the panel with my father and uncle standing close by. The Chair of the Magistrates or whoever it was in charge spoke a few words, most of which I didn't understand or chose not to.

I was then asked a question by the Chair. Of all the conversations I had experienced and all the questions asked of me to that point and indeed to this day, this question I believe had such a pronounced affect on me that I can still feel the fear, confusion and utter disbelief of what was being asked of me. It was a fairly simple question:

My father, taken in 1972.

"John, who would you like to live with, your father or your Aunt and Uncle?"

I was somewhat at a loss. My aunt and uncle had given me stability and love for the last three years, they had pulled my life around and given to me a feeling of worth and belonging, I had almost in that short spell of my life come to think of them as my mother and father. And then there was my father standing beside me looking at me waiting for the answer.

If I replied "my father", I felt I was letting my aunt and uncle down, almost saying – well thanks for the last three years, but time for me to go now. I did not want to go, I did not want to leave them. However, my father was my father and I did not want to let him down, maybe there existed within me a fear that if I rejected him now I might not see him again.

I don't know why or the real reasons as to my decision, neither do I know if I even made the right decision, what I do know is, my heart sank and I felt despair when I replied "my father".

I wish the court had made the decision for me, I felt really sorry for my uncle, I felt I really had let him down. He had to return home to my aunt and tell her I had gone and I would not be returning home to her. I remember him patting me on the back of my head, almost a gentle stroke, no words were ever spoken he simply walked out and left me there.

People often ask of me – if you had the chance again, and knowing what you know now, would you have made the same decision? The answer is – I still don't know. I made the decision with the heart of a child.

Now as an adult, being asked the same question again? Maybe I would have stayed with them, but then so much of what has happened to me in my later years since I left, has been so fulfilling and rewarding, that fate dictates it was the right decision.

What I can say is, the following years were not altogether happy years for me, I missed living with my aunt and uncle and the promises my father made never materialised, in fact the day he took custody of me, he left me!

My father did not take me to my grandparents following the court case. He said he had to go somewhere, instead he got a friend of his to "drop me off". His friend took me in a sidecar attached to a motorbike and left me to wander in to say "hello" to my grandmother.

My grandparents had since moved from the house they were living in on the Old Park Farm Estate, it had become too large for my grandmother to cope with.

There is a funny story surrounding that move. My grandfather had become very fond of the old house, his local the Hare & Hounds was just a short walk up the hill. He had no intention of moving home and so adamant was he to stay put that on the day of the move, he remained in a single chair my grandmother had left for him.

My grandmother was determined to leave and set up home at Laurel Road so she simply left him there! A little while later he upped sticks and joined her but he still continued for many years to make the journey to the pub, one night a week and always on a Sunday to play dominoes and crib.

On the day of my arrival at my grandparents, my grandmother was there to receive me, I believe she had retired at this point but my grandfather still had a few years remaining. She made me welcome and explained I would be going to a new school just around the corner from where they lived, the Bishop Milner.

She went on to explain that when I came home from school I would be expected to run down to the shops and collect a few groceries and the evening paper and she would have a cup of tea waiting for me.

I remember this time very well, it would have been July 1966. I know this because it was during the six week school closedown, I was all set to go to Mons Hill School but my grandmother changed this and I remember sitting with my father, grandmother and grandfather watching England beat Germany in the World Cup Final on a black and white television.

I quite clearly recall my aunt Sylvia (my father's sister) taking me to town to buy my new school uniform, trousers, shirt, blazer, tie and a school badge. Hooray! Long trousers at last!

My life at Laurel Road was fairly uneventful at first, the obvious difference was that I had been separated from my mother's side of the family. From the day I arrived at my grandparents it was to be ten or eleven years before I next met her again.

When I say my life was uneventful! I recall the early days of having to go to the shop, pick up the evening newspaper and a few groceries, a loaf or maybe a bottle of milk. During my visits to the shop about two hundred yards down the street, I began to get taunted by a group of local lads who obviously knew each other well, had probably formed an alliance and saw me as "easy meat".

Every night they would wait for me, let me get to the shop and then on my return chase me, hell for leather up the street. My ability to run fast meant I could always outrun them and made it to the safety of my grandmother's house. There was one particular lad who always seemed to be at the forefront of the group, maybe because he was the fastest or fancied his chances of giving me a beating.

This continued for a week or two, each time I evaded them. Then one evening I had a particularly heavy grocery bag, so off I went with the group in tow. I ran as fast as I could but the weight of the bag was slowing me down, I realised that this time I wasn't going to make sanctuary. I got to within ten yards of the house and this particular lad had caught up with me, on my shoulder with his breath on my neck.

I decided I had to stop, turn and confront him. I had a decision to make, I was either going to allow this to continue on an almost daily basis and run the risk of taking a beating each time or confront this head on.

I got stuck in and as we dragged each other across the middle of the road I managed to roll him over onto his back, I pinned him down by sitting on his chest and just as I was about to punch his lights out, there was my grandmother, pulling me off him telling me, "Bloody little sod, you've only been here five minutes and you're fighting, causing me trouble!"

All my efforts of trying to explain it wasn't entirely my fault fell on deaf ears, literally. Following that skirmish the lads welcomed me, seems I came through the initiation and we became very good friends, daily visits to the shop became uneventful.

I had a really good friend in 'Shandy', but the problem was he was so embarrassing. His hair was so long it hung over his eyes and when he walked he had a habit of walking sideways, very funny to watch. One day we went for a walk over the local park and in the centre of this park was a very large and dirty pool. I made my way towards a bench on the far side whilst Shandy took in the trees and the squirrels. Realising I wasn't around he ran as fast as he could towards me, not seeing the pool and falling straight in, it took me ages to pull him out and boy did he stink.

I took him home and bathed him, Shandy was my mongrel dog.

As the days progressed I began to settle into my new surroundings, new friends and a new school, but I became more and more concerned that I had not seen my aunt and uncle. I had left them without so much as a goodbye or a hug, I never had the opportunity to say thanks, not that they would have wanted that.

I decided one day to go and pay them a visit, one day became another and before long I was becoming a regular visitor. I had to keep my visits a secret from my grandmother knowing full well she would have prevented me from going. Then, due to my naivety, one day I suggested to Stephen that he could come with me to visit.

Boy, was that a mistake! Stephen must at some point have been put under pressure to divulge where we had been to, he eventually cracked and had to "tell". My life was made a misery from that point on, my aunt (my father's sister) with whom Stephen was living, suggested to Stephen that I was a bad influence on him and he had to keep away from me.

I got a roasting from my father and grandparents and was told in no uncertain terms that I was no longer allowed to visit my aunt and uncle, I had to keep away "in case I bumped into my mother", that was one of the reasons I was going over there, though to be fair I never did "bump into her". In fact at this point in time I lost all contact with her.

From that moment on Stephen's visits to my grandparents were always in the company of my aunt, so as not to forward me the opportunity to "influence" him. So I decided if I was to become a rebel, I had to go it alone. I continued to visit my aunt and uncle on a regular basis from then on in total secrecy.

I never did really settle at Laurel Road, my father was hardly ever there, he had met another woman and as par for the course was working away from home a lot. He came back occasionally and I had to share my bed with him, not the best arrangement for a teenager.

I can't be sure but I always had the distinct feeling that my grandmother never really wanted me living with her. If on the odd occasion, as teenagers do, I stepped out of line I would be told that my father was not paying anything towards my keep and until I was eighteen I could always be put back into the children's home.

I felt like a child that was on loan. Well, you try him for a little while, see how things go and if it doesn't work out you can send him back. I often sat and wondered where my life was going. Where would I be next year, the year after that?

The stability of family life and the comfort one must get from feeling wanted and belonging, which was so lacking in my life was further compounded one Christmas when my grandmother said to me, "Your granddad and I are going to spend Christmas day with your aunt Sylvia. I don't know what you're going to do."

I felt so rejected and alone at that point, was no one in this family going to show me just a little compassion? Didn't anyone love me, or want me? I was going through adolescence, very fast it seemed to me, so I made the decision that when the time was right I had to get away from this family.

I made a conscious decision that I would apply to join the Royal Marines and spend the rest of my life living independently away from all this bitterness and rejection. If I was to be alone then it would be on my terms. Fate however dictated that that was never going to happen.

My time at secondary school was fun and I made friends, I tried to learn as much as I could but because of my earlier lack of education and late start I was always playing catch up. I took part in the school football team and became quite good at athletics, making the English Schools Team at cross country running.

I was also involved, in fact instrumental, in putting together a project on The Black Country. My claim to fame is that during my final year at school, as part of this project we had to 'dig out' a set of furnace bellows from a nail shop down at Halesowen. These very bellows now take pride of place in the nail shop at the Black Country Living Museum.

The "Caves" football team. My father is second from the left. Notice I am in the centre front holding the ball. This is one of the teams my father managed over a period of many years. I later played for this very team in the "Dudley & Cradley Heath League".

My efforts to educate myself and make something from this catastrophe called childhood, led me to the third level in my year, I never quite made the primary level where the swots sat, but I was happy where I was.

The time came for me to start to make decisions concerning my life after school, my career. I knew that in order to get into the armed forces and in particular the Royal Marines I would need to sit O Levels and obtain decent grades. So I was all set to stay on at school and move into the sixth grade, work hard, sit my exams and see what transpired. However, once again my family had other ideas.

My grandmother decided in her wisdom that I was not staying at school any longer and I needed to leave and get a job. Her reasoning for this was that she had kept me (looked after me) for four years, had no financial support from my father, therefore it was time for me to support myself.

It was strange she should say that because in some ways I had supported myself from the age of thirteen. I obviously wasn't getting any pocket money from my grandparents and certainly not from my father. So I answered an advertisement in the local newspaper asking for a school kid to help out at the local newspaper office five nights a week for a couple of hours and all day Saturday.

It only involved cleaning a couple of printing machines, cleaning the vans on Saturday and running a few errands. For those eighteen hours I received the princely sum of thirty shillings, £1.50 in today's money. It allowed me however to do the things my mates were doing, buying records etc.

One Christmas my grandmother asked me what I would like for Christmas. I replied "a pair of shoes might be nice". She asked me to get me a pair and she would give me the money. So off I went and bought myself a pair, showed them to her and received the acknowledgement they were ok, but never got the money for them. That year I bought my own Christmas box.

Anyway, the business of leaving school. I was really gutted that I was being denied this chance to get the qualifications that would help me and although I pleaded with my grandmother to let me stay on at school, and the head teacher was keen to see me stay, my grandmother sent my aunt Joan to the school. The fact my grandmother was stone deaf omitted her from the discussion.

It was obvious my aunt was primed with all the reasons I should leave, I had no say in the matter, once again decisions were being made about my life I had no control over. So I was resigned to leaving school at the age of fifteen at Easter 1970.

Such was my resolve and determination that I was not going to get a dead end job for the rest of my life I decided to rebel slightly. Unknown to my grandparents and their family I was still in contact with my aunt Alice and uncle Jack, visiting as often as I could. My uncle Jack and uncle Ted both worked as labourers at a local engineering company so I asked them to make enquiries as to whether I might be taken on as an engineering apprentice. I had little hope due to the fact that most apprenticeships required the candidate to hold O Levels.

However my uncles did a splendid job convincing the training officer to give me an interview. I went along, did a few tests and was offered a job as a mechanical engineering apprentice. I let my grandparents believe it was all my own work, had I told the truth I would have been scuppered.

I left school on Friday following the Easter shutdown and began working on the following Monday. Due to the early start date I spent the following six months working on the shop floor before entering the twelve month programme in the company's training school.

My determination not to accept the inevitability of leaving school without qualifications and moving from one boring job to the other did have a price. Because I was an apprentice on an apprentice training programme I earned little money. My first wage amounted to 110 shillings (£5.50). I had been given quite graphic and explicit instructions by my aunts (my grandmother's daughters) that when I received my first wage packet and subsequent ones, I was not to open them but to hand them over to my grandmother who would take out her

This is my grandmother taken on my wedding day, looks happy doesn't she?

'house keeping' or 'board money' as it is sometimes called and give me back my 'pocket money'.

So having received my very first wages in a small brown envelope, I handed it to my grandmother. Naively I thought she would take a small percentage and give me the rest. Boy was I wrong! She took £4.00 and gave me thirty bob (£1.50) back.

So there I was contemplating having worked part-time for two years after school and Saturdays, clocking up eighteen hours and earning £1.50, I was now working 40 hours earning the bloody same!

To add insult to injury I was then told, "Now you're working you can buy your own clothes and shoes." This family really knew how to kick the s**t out of you.

I found out the results of my City & Guilds exams from my grandmother, she would open all my mail arriving at the house, knowing full well it had my name on it. She opened all my mail, read it and told me the contents!

The only thing that kept me sane and determined to carry on was my sheer stubbornness to make something of my life despite the continuing knock backs.

SEVEN

Love

A YEAR after starting work, in the April of 1971, on Thursday the 15th to be exact, an event was to happen that would change my life forever, change my attitude and set me on a new life course.

My 'Doughnut' arrived! No! I hadn't discovered masturbation. My family and some of my friends will know precisely what I mean, but for the uninitiated let me explain.

Over the last six years or so previous I had built up quite a little circle of friends, some close, some not so close, my best mate was a guy name David, Dave for short. Dave had a couple of cousins, Anthony and Steve. We also made good friends with a lad name Eddie. We spent most of our time playing football over the local playing fields and usually at night we would spend time either at Dave's or Anthony's house.

Most of our leisure time was taken up with listening to records we had bought or playing a league of Subbuteo (the table top football game). I never took my friends back to my grandmother's they were never made to feel welcome, she would offer some criticism aimed at me and enquire if they did the same things! It seemed to me that she would find any opportunity, anything to embarrass me.

Laurel Road was never a home, merely a place for me to sleep. My grandmother was forever cooking meals I detested, dishes of conger eel, heart, pig's feet, pig's tail, brains, tripe and rabbit.

On one occasion when I walked in, she had prepared a stew or casserole of some concoction. My granddad was just finishing his meal in the kitchen when she asked me to sit down, my grandfather got up and moved into the front room to watch the TV, she then lifted up his plate and began to serve the stew on it placing it in front of me, expecting me to eat it! She moved into the front room and the stew promptly went into the bin.

I began to lose my appetite quite quickly over the coming months and resorted to popping into the local café within the town centre after finishing my little part-time job, this would be about six thirty or so each evening of the week. I loved the egg, sausage and chips they served there, although it did get a bit monotonous, it was better than facing a plateful of conger eels or a dish of brains.

This one particular Thursday night I referred to earlier, I was feeling pretty low and had been discussing with Dave my intention of leaving my grandparents home and joining the Marines. I really felt I was not welcome there, despite the fact they had taken me in and cared for me, I felt they did it for my father, not for me or because they were concerned about me. So with nothing else to do that evening we were kicking a ball across the road to each other and generally just messing about.

I noticed out of the corner of my eye two girls walking down the street towards us. I didn't pay much attention and as I turned around and kicked the ball across the street it hit the one girl, I did feel a bit of a plonker and apologised to her. All I remember saying at that point was "I'm sorry" and getting some sort of reply such as "it's ok!".

When I gazed at her that first time I guess my hormones must have kicked in from somewhere, she was the most amazing vision I had ever seen. Her long shining dark hair and hazel eyes totally bemused me, there was something about the way she walked, the way she stood, so petite and yes I know it sounds like a song, but seriously, I was besotted by her. There I was staring at the girl who would become my wife, Diane.

Those people I have come to know over the years, who I have debated with and who say there is no such thing as love at first sight, they argue that love has to be built, that it is something that gradually arrives, built not simply on looks, but on personality. And what we think is love is in fact infatuation, lust! I disagree. Maybe Jacob Black understood it when he said:

"It's not like love at first sight, really. It's more like gravity moves. When you see her, suddenly it's not the earth holding you here anymore. She does. And nothing matters more than her. And you would do anything for her, be anything for her. You become whatever she needs you to be, whether that's a protector, or a lover, or a friend, or a brother."

(Source) Eclipse (Twilight #3) Stephanie Meyer Published May 31st 2008 by Little, Brown and Company (first published August 7th 2007).

I fell in love at that moment in time and I still get butterflies when I look into her eyes now. She continued to walk to the shop where she was going with her friend and I just had to convince Dave to ask her to go out with me, pleading with him to stop her on the way back and invite the both of them on a date.

Dave wasn't very cooperative he wasn't very keen on going out with her friend, but agreed he would do this one thing just the once for me, then I was on my own. So, just as they were coming back I made a quick exit, such was my embarrassment I didn't want to be there when he asked the question.

I gave him a few minutes, realising he would need time himself to pluck up the courage and then decided to go out and say hello myself, hoping that he had sorted out this date. I walked down the path towards the two girls with a doughnut in my hand, I guess psychologically I needed something to do to hide my shyness. Hence her nickname 'Doughnut', something that has stuck for over forty years.

Anyway, they went on their way and I asked Dave if he had asked them? And yes! He had arranged we would meet the both of them at seven thirty on the corner the following night. The next twenty-four hours became intolerable for me, wondering if they had just said yes to get away or were serious about the meeting. The following night I spruced myself up and waited with bated breath for them to appear. Eventually they arrived, it was raining steadily and fortunately they had umbrellas. So we spent a couple of hours walking around and I think at some point I held her hand.

It might appear to outsiders that I am being corny, however, I knew at that moment, on that night that this girl would be a part of my life forever. We spent the next two years or so being together, every minute I had spare was spent with her.

My grandmother, as I expected did not approve of the relationship, although there is just fifteen months between our ages, me being older, the fact that I had to leave school earlier than I would have liked and Diane stayed on to sit her exams, she held the view she was "just a school girl". I ignored the constant comments and rebuffs and carried on seeing her.

Even through our early relationship my grandmother continued to embarrass me. One night we were standing outside the gate of Diane's house, just a fifty metre distance from where I lived. My grandmother came toddling up the road at about nine-thirty, bearing in mind I was about seventeen at this point, and said: "It's about time you were in the house chap." Diane laughed the episode off, but I found it wholly embarrassing, I think my grandmother probably did that simply to demonstrate she was in control.

Whatever comments were made they never changed my mind about how I felt about Diane, I fell in love and nothing was going to change that. Diane was the first person I can ever recall ever saying to me, "I love you". I can clearly remember asking if she understood what she was saying, I guess I needed that reassurance that it wasn't simply something that perhaps needed to be said at that particular time, but that it was a real statement of commitment and sincerity and that I was someone she really did care about and wanted to be with. No one, not even my mother or father had ever said that to me.

For the first time in my life I had found a person I genuinely felt at ease with, someone who actually did love me for who I was, someone I felt would not threaten me and a relationship that was built on love, trust and understanding.

During the initial two years or so we were together we made many plans. We were going to get married and at some point have children and live happily ever after. We even decided on the name of our first child!

Those two years I have to say were amongst the happiest in my life, all I did, all I thought about was Diane and I couldn't wait to be with her during each and every day. Her parents almost became my adopted parents, they welcomed me into the family and have over time treated me as their own son and I have come to treat them as my mother and father.

It was Diane's mother, who when she found out I was to spend Christmas on my own, invited me to spend Christmas with them, Diane, her mother and father, her sister and two brothers. I had Christmas lunch with them but as her mother came from the kitchen with the bowls of trifle on a tray and said, "Would you like some trifle John?" She then proceeded to drop it into my lap, I can't remember who was more embarrassed.

My relationship with Diane and her family continued to grow and get stronger and stronger over time. Our plans however, were inadvertently redesigned. Diane found out she was pregnant and after dealing with the early trauma of telling her parents, like a coward I left that to her, while I told my grandmother who simply said "I'm not surprised".

We made plans for the wedding. The initial planning for the ceremony was something of a farce given that I was Catholic and Diane was Church of England. We decided to approach the local Catholic priest at the church which I spent most of my childhood visiting. Taking into consideration I hadn't been to church since I left school, I was somewhat apprehensive about going along to the vicarage to discuss wedding plans.

I thought the vicar is bound not to recognise me and refuse to marry us, it seemed to me whilst growing up and going to a Catholic school, that if for some reason you didn't turn up for Mass on a Sunday, the vicar always knew about it and would confront you in front of the whole class on a Monday morning, he seemed to have this uncanny knack of remembering everyone, hence my apprehension.

However, I was pleasantly surprised by his good nature and on the evening we both attended my fears were soon to disappear, especially as we began to talk. Diane was at this time around two to three months pregnant, so we began to talk about the ceremony and the fact that Diane was not Catholic and we needed to sort out the wedding banns and all else that goes before getting married in a Catholic church.

All was going splendidly well, until the vicar said, "We are probably looking at early next year then?" At this point my heart leapt into my mouth because I was hoping to all intents and purposes to keep the impending birth in the background. Catholic priests, bless their hearts do not like the fact that their flock have been playing mommies and daddies outside of wedlock. Now I could have been really cheeky and asked for a double booking, the wedding and the christening over the same weekend?

However, I had to come clean and basically say, "Sorry Father, we can't actually wait that long." Now with him being quite astute and noticing my knees knocking together with beads of sweat running down my forehead, he then went on to say "Right then, that being the case you will have to seek permission from the Archbishop." To which I replied, "How long will that take?" Are you beginning to see the funny side of this? Because I was having visions at this point of us having to go and visit the Archbishop with the baby in tow!

Needless to say we declined the invitation to take it any further and made arrangements to see the local vicar at the local parish church (Church of England) who was only too glad to marry us, bump an' all.

I have to say that my aunt Sylvia did help us quite a lot with the organisation, the time we had to plan was scarce but we managed to get things together and

Our Wedding Day.

in August 1973 we got married at a local church with virtually all the families present.

My best man on the day was my mate Dave (think I might have mentioned that), we took along our own stereo system and records to a local pub and had a fantastic night, dancing to amongst others, Donny Osmond and "Young Love".

During the evening's festivities my grandmother Fisher sat with her daughters, my aunts and uncles etc. I realised at some point during that night that I would not be going back to Laurel Road and my grandparents, there was never an offer for us to live there, but I felt grateful for the time I had been allowed to stay. I went over to my grandmother, sat down in front of her and said, "I love you!"

That for me was my way of saying thank you for taking care of me these last seven years and it came from my heart. She looked glaringly at me with no emotion whatsoever in her eyes and turned away.

We spent our early months of marriage living with Diane's grandparents from her father's side. Our first son arrived in January 1974, and was named Lee. He was actually due on Christmas Day, but Diane went a week over and the doctor in his wisdom decided to book her into hospital and induce her on New Year's Day. So I spent that New Year's Eve on my own feeling sorry for myself, but full of anticipation and excitement in readiness for our new arrival.

Although Diane's grandparents looked after us and we were happy being there together, eventually we had to move on and were fortunate after a short stay at Diane's parents, to be offered a house of our own, the three of us moved in as a family to a place we still live in to this day.

During the later part of 1973 early 1974, I realised the job I had at Ewarts (which at the time stood at Burnt Tree Island, now occupied by the new Tesco superstore) and especially earning the salary of an apprentice was insufficient to look after my family, I needed to increase my income.

Lee.

Diane's uncle worked at John Thompsons, known as Rockwell International Ltd, a company within walking distance of where we lived. He was able to pull a few strings, get me an interview and I managed to convince the Personnel Officer to take me on as an apprentice and complete my apprenticeship, both at college and at a training centre in Digbeth for a period of about one year.

I worked in the tool room and my salary doubled with immediate effect. I spent five years in total at college and by the time I reached 21 I had qualified as a tool room technician with all the qualifications I needed.

We spent our time enjoying our new baby and the new house, getting things around us and settling down as a new family. Like most couples we visited the in-laws when we could, but I never felt happy visiting my grandmother, she never made us feel welcome and I always felt out of place, a throw back from my time living there I guess!

Since moving to live with my grandparents in 1966, I had no contact with my mother, I had no idea where she had gone or who she might be with. At one point I had been told she had died, but that's all I was told. Then, during the later stages of Diane's second pregnancy my aunt Alice sent a letter over to me via a messenger simply stating 'could I call to see her'.

When I went over, she asked me if I knew where my mother was? Of course the whole thing came like a bolt out of the blue, I told her as far as I was aware my mother was dead. She then informed me that for the last ten years she had been a resident in Monyhull Hospital, a hospital for the mentally sub-normal over in Birmingham.

Apparently she had gone over to Birmingham for reasons known only to her, she was heavily pregnant at the time and had been living in the neighbourhood of Ladywood. However, she had given birth to a baby girl and then transferred back to the hospital where she continued to stay and the child had been taken away from her. She had told the hospital authorities she had no immediate family and did not wish for anyone to know where she was.

Had her health been fine my guess is I would never have found her. Her health had in fact deteriorated to such an extent that my aunt had been informed via a letter the hospital had sent to her brother, (my uncle Ted), that she was dying of cancer and had approved contact with the family.

I informed Stephen who himself was married at this point of my discovery and the four of us, Stephen, myself and our two wives, Diane and Sandra went to visit her. When I walked into the hospital ward and saw her lying in her bed, I had a vague recollection of her, but the woman before me was not the woman of stature and strength I remembered.

It must have been some twelve years since I had last seen her, I remember trying to visualise through her face and her hair the mother I had left behind all those years ago, but it seemed to me to be two different women. The cancer had done its job and taken away the beauty I had once so admired. She was not prepared and neither was I for the lifetime separation.

I had missed so much, her love and comfort, her protection and her fortitude, and there was nothing I could do to retrieve it. She had lost so much weight, yet still managed to jump up out of bed at one point, frightening Stephen's wife, Sandra half to death.

The strange thing about this visit was the fact that all the time we were there, she continually kept pointing towards the bottom of the bed with her finger saying, "Who's that little girl?"

We visited her on one more occasion before I was awoken in the early hours of November 4th 1976, by two police officers informing me of her death at Monyhull. I asked the police if they would inform Stephen and my father who were living and working in Pontypridd, Wales at the time.

The following day our daughter was born, a baby girl (Carlene) and as one might expect we were over the moon at that point in our lives, however, fate was to deal me a cruel hand yet again. November 1976 was to be a month I would never forget for the rest of my life. During those early days of the month I was torn between rejoicing at the birth of our daughter Carlene, and remorse for the loss of my mother.

I visited Monyhull one more time along with my mother's sister (aunt Mary). No one on either side of the family had offered financial assistance to arrange the burial of my mother, therefore I took it upon myself to do that, I felt it was the least I could do for her. The hospital staff handed over the few belongings she had, a rosary, a legacy of her Catholic faith and a couple of rings she had worn, one or both were handed to Stephen's daughter for safe keeping.

I arranged the funeral and it took place over in Dudley where she had spent most of her life. My uncle Ted (her brother) allowed the cortege to leave from his house and my mother was buried on the 10th of November, at Dudley cemetery on the Catholic side.

I went back to Monyhull many years later as part of my family research, to establish how my mother arrived there and the circumstances surrounding the birth of Susan. I was afforded the opportunity to speak to the Psychiatrist responsible for my mother's care during her stay at Monyhull. He informed me she had arrived at the hospital through the following process.

She had arrived in Birmingham and had been befriended by a man known as Mr Campbell, he apparently met her at New Street Station, though I don't believe this was a pre planned event. It appears they lived together for a short time in the back to back houses in Ladywood, he took my mother to the hospital for sexually transmitted diseases. It was following this visit that she was transferred to Monyhull, obviously the authorities were concerned about her wellbeing and I assume the health of the baby. One month later whilst a resident at Monyhull she gave birth to Susan, her final child. She went back to Monyhull where she stayed until her death.

The final notes on her file, a shortened version I had been handed, stated that whilst at Monyhull she made many friends and had a job which allowed her some independence and her epilepsy, which initially appeared whilst she was pregnant with me, was brought under control by drugs. In fact, she had only one fit whilst she was there.

You would imagine following the end of her life on this earth that would be the end of any bitterness and friction which existed between the families and finally my mother could rest in peace. But once again, my father's family were to demonstrate just how cruel they could be.

Five days following my mother's funeral, our baby daughter had fallen seriously ill, unknown to us or anyone else she had been born with a defective aorta (the main artery to the heart). She had been 'off the hooks' so to speak for a couple of days not seeming to want to take her feeds, on the evening of the 14th I had fed her and placed her on my shoulder to wind her at which point she threw it all back.

The following morning the Midwife came to visit and Diane explained her concern, I was at work. The nurse noticed that the baby's feet were blue and suggested the doctor be called. The doctor did call but felt all was well, but when I arrived back that evening I wasn't happy with what I had heard and neither was Diane.

We called the doctor out again and this time he said, "You can take her to hospital if you wish, but they might want to keep her in." We both agreed it was better to take her, if only to satisfy our minds that all was well. The doctor made a call and arranged for us to take her over to New Cross Hospital at about 7pm that evening.

I can still see her bright little eyes peeping over the blankets in her carrycot as I walked through the corridors, looking up at me almost as if to say "help me daddy". We waited in the hospital whilst the doctors and nurses did what they could, they had informed us fairly quickly that she was very poorly.

I recall going outside with Diane's father for a smoke and saying to him "I can't lose her" I broke my heart that night because I sensed I was going home without her. There was nothing anyone could do to help her and following her baptism at the hospital she passed away peacefully before midnight that evening of November 15th.

Was Carlene the little girl my mother had seen at the bottom of her bed that day?

I remember having to carry the empty carrycot out of the hospital, place it in the car and make our way home, leaving her there. When I got back home Diane's sister was there waiting, she had been babysitting Lee and had no idea of the seriousness of the problem, I remember telling her "she's gone".

I then did something I have come to regret since. I began collecting up all Carlene's things her clothes, her bottles, her toys and moving them out the way. I think at the time I did it because I didn't want Diane to see them, it was as if I needed to remove them to save her the pain, to remove the things that reminded her of Carlene.

I was so naive and she asked me why I was moving everything? I think she thought I was trying to pretend she hadn't been here. We do the most extraordinary things when we grieve, we have so many confusing thoughts and questions running through our minds that sometimes we forget there are others around us, close to us, that are also confused and in pain and the last thing we should do is add to that grief.

I realised at that moment what I was doing was attempting to erase the memory of our daughter in the eyes of my wife. I promptly put everything back.

I visited my grandmother a day or so later to break the news to her, only to be greeted with the comment, "Never mind, you'll get over it!" I still wince today at her cold shoulder approach to life and human emotion. This was to be demonstrated further when I informed her of the date for the funeral of our little girl a few days later when I revisited, I was sitting opposite her at Laurel Road when she made the startling statement:

"Your aunties and I were going to send some flowers, but as you are having her buried with your mother we have changed our minds!"

I should reiterate that my mother's funeral had been financed by myself and was fairly expensive even back then, in fact I paid for it over a number of months so I simply could not afford to purchase another plot and why should I not bury my daughter with her grandmother?

They had never met and my mother had never hurt any one of her children intentionally, I wanted them to look after each other, after all Carlene was merely a tiny baby who had so little life on earth, I wanted someone to look after her where ever she was in the afterlife. The fact my grandmother could use my daughter as a weapon against my mother now she was dead was simply the last straw. I said nothing, I walked away and I never saw my grandmother again.

Carlene was buried on the 23rd of November and had an abundance of flowers from her family. I bitterly regret not taking a photograph of her, I believed I had more time. My grandmother died in June 1983 aged seventy-five, I found out about her death a few weeks following her funeral from my father, who inadvertently forgot to mention it.

It's strange, I didn't feel anything, I didn't want to cry, didn't need to cry and then I realised why. This is what she had done to me, she had ripped the emotions and any feelings I had for her out of my heart over the past few years and there was really no need to have done that. I hadn't done anything wrong, my mother's faults and failings were not mine, I had no control over that, I just wanted to be a child and to be loved like a child, but they allowed me to grow into an adult feeling bitter, resentful and empty.

Had they all failed to realise or even notice that all those years before when I was growing up, I had been hurt, rejected and pushed from pillar to post, continually told: "You will go back to the children's home if you don't behave."

I just wanted to be loved and accepted by my family by those near to me, they allowed their prejudices to cloud their hearts and thus cloud mine. I held out my arms so many times, only for them to turn away and thus push me away. What a waste!

I did go and visit my grandfather Fisher just once before his death in 1987, I owed him that and I'm glad I did, it allowed me closure with him, I loved him and respected him for allowing me to be part of his life. Then I guess that should be a given, but the way I felt it was more a grateful acknowledgment.

I spent some of my life 'thanking' people (some of them strangers at the time) for looking after me, for caring for me, foster parents, relatives. We shouldn't have to say "thank you for taking care of me", not children.

For the next eight years I was to put the events of 1976 and all those years before, to one side. We had two more sons during that time (Craig and Christopher). I was determined to give my children a quality of life I never had, I would take care of them, protect them, give them a decent education but above all I would love them and always be there for them, for as long as they needed me. And I would tell them as often as they needed to hear it, "I love you".

I was determined to take care of my wife, to love her and treat her with the dignity and respect that a marriage demands, I was not going to allow my family to be split up, separated and forgotten, not this family, not now.

I watched my children grow and mature, I saw the happiness in their faces and the delight they exuded at birthdays and especially at Christmas time when they opened their presents. Diane always made Christmas a family affair and went out of her way to make it special. For me, Christmas was never anything

Craig.

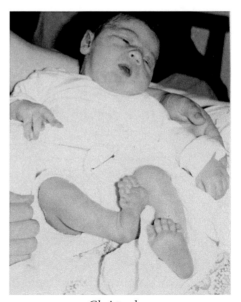

Christopher.

special, I had very little experience during my childhood and I guess that reflected in my attitude towards it, even today. However, I never allowed it to show and joined in the celebrations.

During my moments of solitude when I had time on my hands, gently simmering away in some distant corner of my mind, were the thoughts of 'Thomas'. How old was he now? Where was he? Was he ok? Was he thinking of me, did he even have any knowledge of me?

I was contemplating my life's journey and could not see a contented and fulfilling life without him, but there existed for all I had then and before me a void in my life, a piece missing that continued to eat away at me. I knew I had to start looking, I had to try and find my little brother.

In 1984 I began a journey that would take twenty-three years to complete. I took the first tentative steps. I set about…

EIGHT

Finding Thomas

THIS IS the second part of my story! Stephen had always supported me in trying to find Thomas though he had little, if any, memory of the past he wanted as much as I to find him.

We therefore decided the best approach would be to go to Social Services and ask for our files, our separate files and the family file. Maybe there would be something in there that would give us a lead as to what happened to Thomas, if we were fortunate they may have inadvertently included information we could use?

We didn't realise at that time, but we had embarked on a slippery slope of bureaucracy and red tape. Social Services had a duty to protect adopted children, there was no way they were going to let us have any information that would lead to Thomas.

I made an appointment to see a case worker, ironically it turned out to be Stephen's very own case worker from years gone by so at least she had some background knowledge of the family.

Knowing what I know today I wish Stephen had come with me to the initial interview, as it was, I went on my own, asking specifically for my records and that of the family. The law dictates that only the person themselves may have access to their own records, and even then with data protection and issues of sensitive information, there is no guarantee that all the information will be handed over. The reason given is that there may have been a teacher at a school who made an unsavoury remark about me. Therefore in order to protect that individual, so I would not go looking for them, the remark would be scrubbed from the record given to me.

I was asked the obligatory questions, why I wanted the information, what I intended to do with it? I explained that the last time I saw Thomas he was about seventeen months old, way back in 1963, that was twenty-one years ago. I had a burning inside me to find him and if I was fortunate enough to find him, to build a lasting relationship. Yes I understood he may not have wanted contact and I could not force that, but to simply know where he was and if he was alright would have been enough for me.

There was also the possibility that Thomas may not have been told he was adopted, then I knew I would have to leave things be, I could not go knocking on his door telling him his parents of the last twenty years or so were not his real parents. Can you imagine the trauma and upset that would have caused for all concerned?

If you're wondering at this point how I knew for certain Thomas had been adopted, well, I got hold of his original birth certificate by simply applying for it through the proper channels of birth, deaths and marriages. On the right hand side of the certificate is the handwritten text 'adopted'.

A few days later, possibly a week, I got the message that my file was now available for me to look at. I was fully expecting to be handed a folder containing lots of information for me to look through, I took along a pencil and paper in expectation of writing what I thought would be important notes.

What I got was one single piece of A4 paper containing bullet points relating to dates in chronological order of the family, children and events from 1960 to 1967. The one thing I did establish at this point was the fact that there were two other children I knew nothing about.

In February 1964, some four months after we all separated for the final time, my mother had given birth to another boy, Mark Edward. I knew my mother had had a baby when she was living at Hillside Road in 1965, but I had no idea whether it was a boy or girl, or what became of the child. There before me was the information that she had given birth to a second baby boy in June and his name? David Trevor! Furthermore she had given birth to a baby girl Susan, born in Birmingham, of all places, in November 1967.

So initially I believed I was one of four surviving children, now there were six of us, four of whom had been adopted. So to clarify the situation – I was born in 1955, Michael in 1956 (deceased), Stephen in 1957, Karen in 1959 (deceased), Thomas in 1962, Mark in 1964, David in 1965 and Susan in 1967.

There was no information that gave any lead or clue about where the children had been placed for adoption, I was completely in the dark as to what to do next. My dilemma was further compounded by the fact that Thomas had changed his surname, or rather his adopted family would have given him their surname. It was also possible not knowing at what age he was adopted that they could have given him a new Christian name. So, I was no longer looking for Thomas Fisher, but a complete stranger in many ways and all I had was his date of birth.

Time began to ebb away once again and events in my life took priority, Diane was heavily pregnant with our fifth child in 1986, Marc Thomas, named after Mark and Thomas but his Christian name ending with a 'C', something he is proud to point out.

But now it was time to take up the mantle once again to find Thomas. This time I decided to go to the head office of Social Services and plead my case. Again I met with a social worker who said she would look at the case files and if there was anything she could help me with she would be in touch. At this point I was clutching at straws.

Then the most extraordinary set of events took place, a set of events that when I tell them, as I have told them to many others in the past, will probably generate the same reaction, you will read, contemplate and disbelieve!

I received a letter from Social Services some two weeks following my visit to them, stating they had some information for me. I was ecstatic, full of beans, could this be the breakthrough I had been waiting for? They stated in their correspondence that they would be in touch shortly to arrange a meeting with me.

I continued to wonder what on earth they had for me, surely they were not going to tell me where Thomas was? Maybe they had come across some information in the

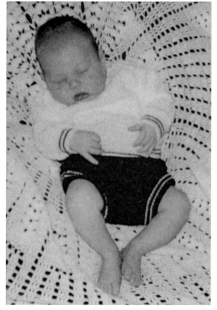

Marc.

file, indicating that he had made a request to be contacted should any member of his birth family make contact?

A few days elapsed and I imagined every possible scenario. I was becoming very agitated, yet excited. What on earth could this news be?

Then one night as I arrived home from work, going about my usual business, the phone rang. Nothing unusual about that.

I picked up the receiver and said:

"Hello?"

A voice on the other end, very calmly said:

"Hello, I'm your brother Thomas."

Imagine my shock at hearing those few words?

My initial instinct was simply to start crying, but at the same time to maintain control of my emotions in order to take in what was happening. My mind was awash with thoughts, was this really Thomas? Was someone playing an awful trick on me? I felt at that moment that I needed to confirm to myself that this really was him.

I can't remember the exact words we exchanged that evening, only fragments of the conversation. I wondered how he had found me? He went on to explain that he knew he had been adopted but knew only of Stephen and not me. He had actually been into the same Social Services office that I had been in, the day after me. I know it seems unbelievable, but yes it is true!

I had been in asking for information about my family and specifically stated I would like to make contact with my brother, I gave them all the details I had at that time and as explained earlier, left to await their contact. The following day Thomas walked in and asked if they had any information on his biological family with the intention of allowing him to make contact.

At that point I can't imagine what the Social Services office must have been like when, as I'm informed, the officer walked upstairs and enquired, "Does the name Fisher mean anything to anyone?" They must have thought it was some kind of prank being played out.

However, the following week little happened due to the fact that Thomas had gone away on holiday, like me, he did not expect things to happen so quickly. When he arrived back home they contacted him, explaining the situation that I had been in touch and wanted to make contact. They gave him my address and contact telephone number for him to ring if he so wished.

As we talked a little more on the phone I recall asking all sorts of questions about his life, as much as I could ask on a telephone. He explained he knew about Stephen because his mother and father had actually fostered Stephen when he was very young.

It now began to make sense as to why Social Services would not give us any detailed information on Stephen, as this would have inevitably led us straight to the door of Thomas's parents. His surname had obviously been changed to that of his adopted parents and his Christian name had changed slightly with a new middle name, but for confidential reasons I won't divulge that information. So for the purpose of this book and so as not to confuse things even further I will relate to him as Thomas.

You will I am sure understand that after all those years of searching for Thomas and having found him now, in one respect I had to let him go and embrace my new brother and get used to his new name.

The telephone call was just that, it was a conversation, I had no idea what he looked like and the same went for him. We conjure up pictures of people on the other end of the phone and invariably they look nothing like we imagine so we agreed to meet up. Thomas felt it better for him to meet with just myself on this occasion, so he could get used to the situation I guess!

We agreed to meet the following evening at a local pub near to me, we agreed the time and of course not having seen each other for over twenty years, how would we recognise each other? Well, we agreed to meet on the pub car park and I described my car to Thomas and vice versa, if that makes sense?

The following twenty-four hours were full of anxiety, uncertainty and of course excitement at the thought of meeting my little brother after all this time. I called Stephen and explained what had happened and he was just as excited as I was.

That following evening I left the house so full of anticipation and trepidation, my heart beating fast, I was shaking a little and my nerves were shot to pieces. I arrived at the pub and vaguely remember parking up, I think I waited just a few minutes and looked around to see if I could identify his car. I do recall thinking "What's he going to look like after all this time, what will he think of me and what do I do?" Do I shake his hand? Which seemed a little formal or do I give him a big hug, which is what I wanted to do or will he feel a little embarrassed about that?

After all I had no idea at this point whether he had any intention of having a relationship, maybe he just wanted to see me, say hello and then goodbye! I prayed this was not going to be the case, not after all this time.

Then I saw a car arrive and this fellow get out, I saw him looking around and kind of worked out this was Thomas. I moved across towards him and said with some trepidation "Thomas?" I think he responded with "John".

All my fears were washed away at that moment as we embraced each other tightly and cried. All those years of waiting were over, all those years of wishing and wondering had finally come to an end. I had found my baby brother, no longer was I going to have to think about "Finding Thomas"! He was here, a physical being, I could finally hold him in my arms, hug him and talk to him.

We spent some time hugging each other and the both of us shed tears. I distinctly remember saying to him that we would have to dry our eyes before going into the pub, heaven knows what onlookers were thinking that night, but you know for me at that very brief moment no one else existed, this was our special moment.

Anyway, we went inside and ordered a drink, sat somewhere fairly quiet and began talking. How do you talk about lost lives, about childhoods that for both of us never existed in terms of us growing up together, sharing those sibling moments, fighting with each other, getting each other into trouble, blaming each other for what the other has done, going on holidays together, spending the long hot summer months building camps and making friends with other kids?

We lost all of that, never to regain it. We had been apart over a fifth of a century, that had now expired, all we could do was relate our memories of those years and imagine what it might have been like to have been there. In some ways I feel bitter having been cheated out of those experiences and shared memories.

My own children often talk about the times of their childhood years when they played together and the adventures they had together. I sometimes listen intently and my heart sinks because my childhood memories and snapshots of play are all about strangers I met during my journey into adolescence.

Thomas and I probably would not have gone to school together due to the age difference of some seven years, however, I would have liked to have been at his wedding. But then I think if we had stayed together within that family structure and environment, our lives would almost inevitably have turned out differently.

When I reflect on my childhood and realise I have four brothers and a sister, and yet I grew up being an only child from the age of eight, my aunt had no other smaller children and my grandparents certainly didn't, how strange it seems.

I don't have a crystal ball and the ability to foresee the future or to return to the past and give life a chance with different circumstances, what we are I believe is in many ways determined by the adults that interact within our lives from a very young age. Given that, I firmly believe that had we not been separated but continued within the family we were born into, we would not be the adults we are today.

This is a subject we did talk about that night, but I was conscious not to suggest to Thomas that I was grateful to his adopted parents or even to suggest that I would like to say thank you to them for looking after him. What they did, they did for their own reasons and as far as they and Thomas are concerned he is their son and they his parents.

I did eventually meet his adopted mother and father, not through a specific invitation, but through a family party that Thomas arranged. I accept that relations are strained and perhaps to his mother and father they find the whole thing difficult, why after all this time have I appeared in his life? What am I seeking? Will I have a detrimental effect on his life?

Maybe if they had spoken to me in the early days they would have had the answers, but now after all this time they must observe that far from a detrimental effect, we have been a necessary part of each others lives. Maybe they perceived that as a child, I came from a dysfunctional family and therefore must be a dysfunctional man?

Anyway, I digress! We carried on talking that night for an hour or two, spoke about our families, my family and Thomas and his family, his wife, his mother and father, his brothers and sisters, some of whom like himself were also adopted. We talked about Thomas waiting a couple of nights before meeting Stephen, his wife and family, my wife and family and introducing us to his wife, however, he decided he wanted to meet Stephen as soon as possible and if I remember correctly I took Thomas to meet Stephen at his home that night.

It transpired later from Social Service notes that had not been handed over initially, that Stephen had stayed with Thomas's adopted parents for a short while in June 1962. Thomas had not yet arrived as a foster child to this address. So, Thomas had been told later on about Stephen but knew nothing of me.

I believe it was the following night or may have been a couple of nights later before Thomas came to my house to meet my wife and we met his, she was very pretty and intelligent but hard work. If that seems abrupt, it is. The less said the better. After a while they separated and eventually divorced, possibly the best thing Thomas ever did.

Thomas had met someone else during this period of uncertainty (Tracy), and he assured me that this relationship was purely platonic during his first marriage and it wasn't until he told his wife things were over that the relationship moved forward.

It appears both Thomas and Tracy were experiencing difficult marriages, both for different reasons and used each other's shoulder to rest on and an ears to listen. He eventually remarried and has a son from that marriage and a daughter from his wife's previous marriage.

I mentioned earlier the difficulties that sometimes arise in situations like this, in relation to parents, biological parents and parents who adopt. When we found Thomas, my mother was no longer alive and therefore not part of the dynamics. My father however was.

He was aware we were looking for Thomas, we had spoken to him on several occasions in an effort to perhaps jog his memory as to what had happened to Thomas and found him to be very vague. He had said that he had made provision for Stephen and me to live with respective aunts on both sides of the family.

He also mentioned he had asked my aunt Sylvia (his sister) to have Thomas, allegedly she had refused, giving the reason for her refusal that my father would interfere. Well of course he would interfere it was his son he was trying to find a home for.

Eventually Thomas disappeared, went into care and spent a little while at Rydal children's home and was fostered out somewhere in the Walsall area. Then around 1966 when he was about four years of age, he was adopted by the family fostering him, the family Stephen had been sent to in 1962.

This explains why Social Services did not hand over this information with the first set of notes, it would have led us straight to the door of Thomas! They handed them over *after* we found Thomas.

I always had the feeling or impression that my father did not seem to pursue the whereabouts of Thomas and did not make an effort to trace him or to keep in touch. I always found it difficult and still do to this day to understand that although the Courts may have issued a care order preventing us three children and the others that were to follow from ever going back to our parents, surely, when deciding on the adoption order, they must have informed my father of the decision or maybe they simply took his son, adopted him out and decided he was not part of the process.

During the times I did speak to my father he made it clear that if we did find the rest of our brothers and our sister he would like to see them, however, if they decided they did not want anything to do with him then he would accept that. I have to admit that there was a time when I thought why should I tell you if I find them? You are their father, if anyone should be looking it should be you.

Stephen and I also made a conscious decision that if we were successful in finding our brothers and sister and they did not want to see our father then we would accept that. We did however contemplate the possibility of them meeting, but having considered the options, we came to the conclusion that we had our lives to lead, our father had his life to lead and so did our brothers and sister. And if through coincidence there should be a meeting, a 'coming together' then we would deal with that when the time came.

The difficulty is imagine if you will a situation where Stephen or I are celebrating a specific birthday and we obviously want to invite our family and friends along. You see where I'm going with this? I want to invite my brothers and I want to invite my father. My brother (and or) my father do not wish to meet each other. Fortunately, in this particular situation we really didn't have such a close relationship with our father (Stephen and I), so the decision was made a little easier.

Thomas, however, complicated matters slightly by suggesting to us that he would like to meet our father but only once and did not want a close relationship with him, which ok, I could come to terms with and accept. However, he also said that whilst he wished to meet my father he didn't want any contact with my father's new family, which consisted of a wife, a son and two daughters. This alienated my father who eventually said, following an initial meeting with Thomas, "If he doesn't want anything to do with my family, then I want nothing to do with him."

Strong words, but understandable.

We continued to be part of each other's lives for many years Thomas, Stephen and I, visiting each other and sharing experiences. The time had come however to move forward and find the rest of our family, now I had another ally, there were now three of us and we would continue this adventure together.

Before doing so though, there was something I needed to do for myself. I had always remembered being fostered out to two families, the one less prominent in my memory than the other. In August 1960, Stephen and I had been fostered to a Mrs ..... (let's call her Smith) at her home in Dudley. I knew where the house was, I had the address from the Social Service file, so I decided to try and track her down, why? To say thank you for letting me into her life for that brief period, it was something I felt I needed to do.

I went along to the house one day and knocked on the door, fully expecting an old lady to answer but it was it was a middle-aged woman, I knew this could not be Mrs Smith, she was middle-aged twenty-five years ago. The woman told me she had no idea who lived there before her and did not know a Mrs Smith, however, if I cared to pop across the road and see Mrs Jones, she had lived in the street all her life and might know who I was looking for.

So across the road I went and yes Mrs Jones did know Mrs Smith! She told me all about her, how long she had lived there, her children and when she left. I asked if she had any idea where Mrs Smith had moved to. Mrs Jones told me she had left the house following her husband's death some years earlier and had gone to live somewhere in Birmingham with her daughter, but had no idea where. My heart sank at that moment, disappointed that I was possibly never going to find her.

Then Mrs Jones exclaimed, "Her son lives around the corner!"

My what a revelation that was, my face must have beamed, she went on to say he was a member of the Salvation Army, like his father. So my next move was to contact the Sally Army, explain I needed to speak to this guy and if I left my phone number would they ask him to contact me.

A day or so later he called me, I explained the situation, my reasons for making contact and my intentions. To be fair to him he fully understood my motives and said he would speak with his mother and get back to me. I waited a while and true to his word, he called me and said his mother did remember me and would like to see me.

A few days later I went over to her address and met up with both her and her daughter, I couldn't remember her features but she remembered Stephen and me arriving at her house. She said that although we were there for just a short time, her recollection of us was one of these two little boys (3 and 5) arriving dirty and bedraggled shouting abuse at everyone.

Every word that came out of our mouths was "f— this" and "f— that". She said the girls (her daughters) thought it was hilarious, they had never experienced anything like that. I spent an hour with her and said goodbye, mission accomplished.

As I explained earlier I had also been fostered in 1962. My mother was pregnant with Thomas at the time and Stephen was fostered with the same family that would eventually foster and then adopt Thomas. On this occasion when I set about going back, Thomas came with me.

We drove to the street I vaguely remembered all those years before, I didn't have the address at this time. I knocked on a few doors enquiring as to whether anyone knew a family that had fostered children years before. No one had.

I got back into the car, believing I had the wrong street and perhaps my memories were not so good. Then just as Thomas started up the engine I said, "Wait, let's give it one more go." I walked up the embankment, knocked on a door and a fellow answered. I introduced myself and said why I was there, I was looking for a family that had possibly fostered children way back in 1962 and that family was name *****.

He asked me to wait a moment, shut the door and came back after a couple of minutes and said, "I think it's my wife you need to speak to." I had indeed found the house, the reason I could not remember it was due to the fact they had replaced the windows and built a porch on the front, not as I remembered it.

Thomas and I spent a half hour or so with my foster mother, her husband had died some years before and she had remarried. She remembered me going there and she still had that multi-coloured blanket I remembered so well. We talked and said our goodbyes, a few months later they moved house, not because of me I hasten to add.

And the irony of all this? A few years later I was to work with the new family that moved into that very house in my capacity as a Neighbourhood Manager, on the exact same estate.

Having put my ghosts to rest it was now time to move on.

NINE

Mark

FINDING MARK was going to be a little more difficult than finding Thomas and would take a further four to five years.

I tried the same approach in that I went to see the social worker who had been Stephens's social worker. She sat in front of me and made it quite clear the name Mark meant nothing to her and she had no idea where he might be!

I knew from his original birth certificate, which I obtained through the local registrar for a few pounds, that he had been born in Wordsley in Dudley, West Midlands on February 24th 1964.

Ironically this was the very same date that Stephen had been transferred to Mr and Mrs Parker (our aunt and uncle, father's sister) as a long stay arrangement, according to the social service records Stephen received. These were the records containing the information about Thomas and his address of future adoption.

By the 17th March an application for revocation of care order, adjourned sine die, by Dudley Juvenile Court saw Stephen remaining with his aunt and uncle as foster parents. Again I see glimpses of this family unprepared to make an effort and with little inclination to increase the wellbeing of humankind in relation to us as a family, unless there was something in it for them.

By taking Stephen as a foster child they would have received a regular income, fine I hear you say, why not? Why not indeed, I reply, but what if the court had refused the application for fostering?

Anyway back to Mark! It was clear to all of us that Social Services were a waste of time and would continue to be so for years to come, rather that assist us in bringing the family together they proved to be a thorn in our side, putting obstacles in the way and simply refusing to cooperate, usually through the lack of two way communication. I think the attitude was, if they ring listen to them, suggest we will be in touch then hang up and forget them!

Therefore we needed a new approach. We thought at the time we could approach a newspaper? Perhaps give them the story of the family and just maybe that would jog someone's memory? Then maybe, just maybe they would have a vital piece of the puzzle. On reflection we didn't want to wash our laundry in public just yet, but a thought for the future.

Thomas came up with the idea of contacting a family researcher, a professional genealogist research service no less! He had contact details for 'Christine' a woman living outside of London who for a set fee would carry out the research for us. She could access the records from places such as the general register office, search limited records (adopted children's index) and make the necessary connections.

So we agreed we would enlist the help of Christine, our very own genealogist researcher. Thomas got in touch with her and gave her all the background details we had for Mark, which as I said earlier was very sketchy. Nevertheless she went away and got on with it.

I must admit that at that point I could not see how even Sherlock Holmes would find him with such limited information and I prepared myself for disappointment and even at this early stage in the process I began to think of our next move, if indeed, Christine had come back empty handed.

Time went on, a few months, and Thomas and his wife Tracy even went down to visit Christine at her home during which time she brought them up to date with progress, which wasn't a lot.

Thomas put me in touch with Christine due to the fact I had all the paperwork and specifically the memory of the family and events. I spoke to her by telephone on a number of occasions, feeding bits of information back and forth. She even asked me in one telephone conversation to attempt to find the location of a woman she was trying to find up this neck of the woods. This was someone who had disappeared from her family and the sister, if I recall, wanted to make contact with her.

So using my new found skills in research, genealogy and plenty of leg work, I did in fact find the woman and as instructed, I left her a letter asking her to get in touch with Christine. I understood as time elapsed that this did in fact happen and the two sisters were reunited. For which we received a discount!

Eventually following a few phone calls from me to Thomas, who called Christine, who then called me, we got something of a result. She said she had narrowed the search down to about five possible names, one of which was a Mark.

Now bear in mind that the adopted parents who had Mark could have changed his Christian name to anything, meaning the name Mark might not be the same person we were looking for.

We, like Christine, assumed that as Mark had been taken straight into care from birth, the likelihood was, due to the underlying fact it had already been decided that the children from this family were never again going to be allowed to live with the birth parents, the local authority would have wanted the adoption to take place very quickly.

We made a judgement call that the adoption probably took place before February 1966, around the age of two, which to be frank is usually the case. That in itself starts to narrow the search criteria down somewhat.

Firstly we were looking for a male, secondly a male from Dudley, adopted locally and if by chance, as many people who adopt tend to do, they retained his original biological birth name, even both original Christian names, Mark Edward! Named after my uncle Ted I assume, he was Edward.

So effectively in terms of the GRO index we were looking for the year and district, or rather that's what Christine was doing, and we were learning the ropes!

It was around this time in May 1989, we agreed to go to the press and we got in touch with a reporter from the local newspaper "The Chronicle". She came along to my house to interview Stephen and myself, we gave her all the details we had and they ran a half page spread on the story, with a very nice photograph of the two of us with all our files and papers spread out in front of us. We never received a positive response in terms of information from the story, but a few people we knew did comment on it.

During the following months time seemed to pass so slowly, Christine kept in touch and kept us up to date with developments, not that there were many. Then one day I seem to recall she telephoned Thomas, I think it was him she called.

She said she had found an entry in the adopted children's register for a Mark, which was close to the entry for Thomas. In fact she said she was chasing up the possibility of the five entries she had informed us of earlier.

Now then, from the thousands of possible entries that could have been Mark we were down to five, not bad! The process I believe Christine used was to order up the adopted birth certificate of the entry she felt was the correct one, if not, then order up the next one. This would have given her invaluable information to move forward. The Christian and surname of the child, the date of adoption, the date of birth of the child, the parent's name and address at the time of adoption plus details of where the adoption took place. If the date of birth is the same as the one you're looking for and the place of adoption close to the original area of birth, well it's worth following up.

The next step is to move forward in time from the birth, say eighteen years to allow for a marriage, so someone born in 1960, might be realistically getting married in 1978. So you search the marriage register for entries in the district you think they may have married and the year you think they may have married.

Remember you're looking all the time for the name of the bridegroom, at this juncture you have no idea of the name of the bride or anything else about her. You then continue till the next year, of course if they don't get married until they are in their thirties, you have a long search and the possibility of many entries.

It appears that Christine found an entry that matched the one she was searching for. She now had a place of marriage, the name of the partner, the name of the parents and more important the address at the time of marriage. This would more than likely be the address of the adopted parents, the address Mark had been living at before he married. He might still be there, having moved his new wife in.

Also, at this stage it is possible to request a copy of the full marriage certificate, which in most instances gives the address of both bridegroom and bride and indeed on this occasion it did! Given the time lapse between the marriage and the time of discovery, there was every possibility the parents would still be at the address.

A quick search through the electoral register would identify the present owners to a specific date. The next step is finding a phone number, at that time the phone book was the best source of information. So here we are with an address and who we think are the adopted parents of Mark.

We have a telephone number and what does Christine do next? Well of course she decides to ring the number! Now, we had no idea at this stage she had moved so quickly in making this match. Last we heard she had a few possibilities to go on but no addresses and certainly no definitive match.

Having established the telephone number was correct to the address and assuming as I said earlier the occupiers had not moved out, she called the number. I never spoke to Christine in any great detail regarding the extent of the conversation she had with Mark's mother, as she was the one who picked up the phone. But yes, this was indeed my brother's home before he married, and yes we had found him!

I'm not aware of what she said to Mark's mother or how she introduced herself, I can only surmise it must have been something of a shock to receive such a call but then, given the circumstances, she must have thought at sometime in the future the call might well come?

I don't know what she must have been feeling at that precise moment. I can only imagine she possibly felt afraid, not for herself but for Mark. Perhaps she thought Mark was safe and settled now after all these years, he had left his biological family behind and had made a new life for himself with the guidance and support of his adopted parents.

And now from out of the murky depths and mists of the past came a call that could take him back, but back to where? The squalor and deprivation the three of us came from was no longer there, we too had moved on and left it behind. But she of course may not have been aware of that.

A leopard cannot change its spots, the notion that things cannot change their innate nature, was I understand something she had possibly been conditioned to believe. I have no doubt that when Mark went to live with his new parents they would have been told something of the family background from the Social Service records. And armed with what I know of those records, I can well understand why someone would stereotype, prejudge and presume for many years later that things could not have changed and naturally you would want to protect your child from that.

And yet, if you have taken a child from such a family and presumably been told the family have separated with the children having been taken into care, some adopted, would you not assume they have had a similar life and upbringing to the child you adopted?

And if one of your friends just happens to be the very social worker involved with this fragmented family and has been visiting you over many years, would you not have been privy to all this information? Maybe the social worker, the very one Stephen and I saw all those years back on two or three occasions, didn't mention any of this on her frequent visits to Mark's home?

Maybe then that is why his mother said he would not want to know his brothers, or have anything to do with his original family! He had been told he was adopted many years before, but it had not been mentioned since.

So what were we to do in a situation such as this? We had made contact with our adopted brother's parent and established that he knew he was adopted, so there was room to move forward now. We were aware that we were not going to cause a major family upheaval by suddenly disclosing to an individual, who has believed all his life his parents were his biological parents were in fact not, and he has a family elsewhere. But he himself has not actually said he did not want contact.

We did not have to ponder this dilemma. Christine decided that there was something not quite right with the conversation she had had previously and decided to try again. But believing she would antagonise Mark's mother or make the situation even more difficult to move forward, she decided to call Mark's in-laws, she had the address from the marriage certificate and found the telephone number.

Now under normal circumstances, she would have spoken to the in-laws to try and establish, if indeed, Mark had ever mentioned his biological family to his wife or made reference to his feelings. But as has become clear by now this search was never going to be straightforward, there would be twists and turns all the way.

When Christine called the number instead of one of the in-laws picking up the phone it was in fact Mark's wife! The in-laws had gone away on holiday and had asked their daughter to watch over the house. She was there at the precise time Christine called and it was she who picked up the phone, in fact she was only intending to be there about an hour before returning home.

Now again I am not sure as to the flow of the conversation, or how Christine got around this one, but the outcome of it was that Mark's wife was indeed aware of the situation in that she knew Mark was adopted and had obviously spoken to him in the past about this, because her view was that Mark would love to meet his brothers.

So when we got the call from Christine, she outlined all that had gone before, but the only bit I recall clearly was, "Your brother would like to meet you." It was at this point once again I felt such a relief coming over me, my eyes filled with tears as the anticipation of being able to see and talk to the brother I had never seen was overwhelming.

Once again as before, I replaced the telephone receiver, went to my wife, hugged her tightly and sobbed uncontrollably in her arms and simply said, "Found him". I think at one point she may even have said jokingly with tears in her eyes, "I don't know about you but I can't keep doing this, how many more?"

I understand that Christine gave Susan, that's Mark's wife, our telephone number and left it to her to tell him that evening on his return from work. Susan believed that Mark deserved to know, had a right to know and would want to know his brothers. Christine's job was done!

Susan plucked up the courage that night to sit him down and break the news to him. In actual fact the way it happened is, Susan had to pick Mark up from a Martial Arts class he had been attending. Mark knew there was something wrong, something not quite right, Susan was behaving somewhat differently.

He asked her what was going on, to which she replied "I'll tell you when we get home." Now Mark being Mark, well he just had to know, he was thinking all sorts of things could be wrong, had someone died? Was Susan about to tell him she was having an affair? So she pulled over in the car and explained that whilst she was at her parents house this woman named Christine had phoned, explained who she was and had told her Mark had some brothers who were trying to get in touch and gave her the phone number of a John Fisher who is your brother, he would like to talk to you. However, you must not tell your mother because she has said you would not want to know.

This must have been one hell of a shock for Mark because up until this moment he had no idea he had brothers from his early life, his life before adoption.

We waited in anticipation for the call to come, which it did at around eight o'clock that evening. From taking the call from Christine to this point had seemed an eternity, however Mark had thought it through for about ten minutes and called.

What on earth do you say to someone you know is your brother who you have never met before? How do you start such a conversation? Well, basically the same as I did with Thomas. How are you? What have you been up to? Well yes, I think that's exactly what we said!

In between the tears flowing down my cheeks, wiping them away from the corners of my mouth and sniffling every few seconds I was handing over the telephone numbers of Stephen and Thomas so he could call them after talking to me and all the time trying to put a face to the voice, to imagine what he looked like. And then back to the arms of Diane for a good old cry and to tell her what he had said and what he thought about all this, she said, "Can we have a break before you set about finding the next one?"

We agreed that the six of us, Stephen, Sandra, Thomas, Tracy, Diane and I would meet up with him and Susan as soon as possible. A few days later, one night in August, we all met up at Thomas's house. We all seemed to arrive before Mark and Susan, maybe it was planned that way so we would be there together?

When Mark walked in Stephen walked out. Stephen was so overwhelmed by the situation and the fact that Mark was so like him I think it shocked him, the situation was all too much emotionally for him to take in.

All this happened around August/September 1989, a time when Susan was half way through her pregnancy. So although Mark and Susan were expecting one new life, they certainly didn't expect the fifteen extras, which were the brothers and all our children.

Mark got to know us all over time and we met his parents at his house some time later, Mark felt it best to tell them he had decided to make contact with us. His mother and father were obviously cautious about the whole situation and as I intimated earlier I can't blame them.

Who wouldn't be having brought up a child from the age of two, nursing him, caring for him, educating him and generally giving him all your love and affection, knowing the background he had come from, wanting to protect him from that, and then discovering 23 years later that family wanted to be part of his life again.

A little while after we met up, when Mark and Susan invited us over to their home to meet his mother and father, I have to say for me it felt like I was at an interview. I think Mark wanted us to meet them to appease any fears they might have had about the relationship and to help them come to terms with those fears or any trepidation concerning our motives.

I remember sitting there in front of his parents and feeling I was being examined, looked over, I knew from conversing with Mark that his father had been in Engineering, something I felt we had in common and in an attempt to break the ice I said to him, "I understand you have been an Engineer?" To which came the solitary response, "Yes." I gave up trying after that. They left within half an hour.

Sometime later, possible years later, Mark and I discussed this initial and only meeting with his parents and he had said that after a day or two had passed his mother had commented to him, "You turned out the best." I don't know how she made that judgement or what she based it on, I think perhaps she was still thinking of the past, rather than looking to the future.

I like to think we proved her fears were unfounded and wished she could have had more time to see us grow together, to see Mark and myself develop a relationship where we can confide in each other, laugh and cry together and share a love that only brothers can understand. Having put this event to one side, we continued to meet and cement our relationships with each other. Mark decided to meet his biological father and that meeting seemed to go well.

Time was moving on now, it had been May 1986 when we met up with Thomas.

This particular journey had taken three years.

The next would span fifteen years.

TEN

David

I DON'T know why it took us so long to instigate the search for the next sibling, David. I guess we were trying to get to know each other, build relationships and in between all of this, like the early days of my life, we all had our own separate lives to live and things to do.

In many ways I regret not having forged ahead to find David, I think of the extra years we could have had together, however, I believe in fate and waiting for the right time.

But we decided we needed to move forward and we needed to find David. So once again armed with Social Service records and the limited amount of information we had, we sat down over many nights and this new found family of mine, drank copious cups of tea and pondered the possibilities.

Could David have been fostered out to one of the foster parents me, Stephen, Thomas or Mark had been to? After all Stephen had! The records seemed not to indicate that and even if he had Social Services would have been wise to the fact and removed any information linking him.

Again and again we talked and surmised if he was like the others, living locally, did he know like the others he had been adopted and had he been told anything of us? Had he tried to search himself? I was back to where I was all those years before, where was he? Who was he with? Was he happy and contented? Time to find out!

David Trevor was born on the 5th of June, 1965 at Rosemary Ednam Maternity Hospital, Burton Road in Sedgley, the same place as me actually! The day was a Saturday, my mother was living at Hillside Road in Dudley at the time of his birth and it was she who registered the birth on the 8th July 1965.

How do I know all this? Because I obtained David's birth certificate, as I did with all the others, applying for them from the information I had obtained from Social Services and like the others, on his birth certificate was the word "adopted".

At the time of David's birth I would be ten and still living with my aunt Alice and uncle Jack. My father was living with my grandmother, but I believe he was seeing another woman, this is quite significant and I will tell you why. Remember Mark had been born the year before David, so there is about sixteen months between these two? And at the time of Mark's birth and registration, my mother and father were recorded on the birth certificate as living at Pitman Street, Kate's Hill. This is the house we were removed from in September 1963 and never returned to our parents.

So here is my mother living at Hillside Road and she has registered my father on David's birth certificate, significant! However, there is a story that exists to this day that the child she had at Hillside Road was black. Now I don't know who perpetrated this particular story and I can't honestly say when I first heard it, but hear it I did and during this search I had fully expected to come across a brother of mixed race.

If you recall, I was told by my aunt Alice that my mother had given birth to another baby, but that is all I was told, I had no idea whether it was a boy or girl. Now it could have been Mark born in February 1964, however, he was not allowed to go back home to Pitman Street, remember the court order issued earlier in 1963? It could also have been David born in June 1965, but he too was taken straight into care. It had to be one of these two children because I was living with aunt Alice at the time, it could not have been Susan, as she was born in 1967, after I left my aunt's. I obviously know it wasn't any of the children born in and prior to 1962, I would have noticed!

I also believe that whilst my mother was lacking in some of her faculties, she would have noticed if one of the children she gave birth to was mixed race, or black, as I was told. Also, I do not think for one minute she would have put my father's name on the birth certificate.

So what was going on here and why would someone make up a story like this? Possibly to discredit my mother's name, maybe it was someone on my father's side of the family who felt they needed to create such a tale to further blight her reputation? Maybe!

But then there is my theory! When the three children were taken into care in September 1963, me being the tender age of 8, I believed my parents had separated. I don't know why I thought this, I just did, maybe because I never saw them again together.

However, it seems that they stayed together at Pitman Street after we left. This is the address on Mark's birth certificate, indicating both mother and father were residing at this address some six months after we left, Mark's birth being registered in March 1964.

And remember, the birth certificate I have for David also shows my father as his father. This birth was registered in July 1965, some 16 months later. The uncanny thing about this certificate is that it shows my father in a different profession. On Mark's certificate he is an engineering labourer, on David's it shows him as being an engineering machinist. Both of these births were registered by my mother. If they were not seeing each other, how did she know?

And furthermore, if they were not seeing each other and she had clearly been seeing someone else and got pregnant by them, why did she put my father's name on the certificate? I believe the truth lies within the two birth certificates, both tell a story, both indicate that my father was still seeing my mother and being intimate right up till the middle of July 1965 and possibly beyond.

So where did the story of the black baby come from? Right then, my father was seeing another woman around 1965, she lived in the same street as my mother, just fifty yards away. The woman in question conceived a child, who is my father's, no one has ever disputed this and I certainly do not. The timeline between the birth of David and the conception of this child is just three months!

If my father was seeing both women at the same time, then it seems to me he would not want his new girlfriend to find out that the wife he was supposedly separated and estranged from was pregnant? It just might make her a little suspicious! So what better way to appease her and throw the suspicion away from him than to declare, "My ex has just had a baby and it is black!" Still to this day the wife who he married after my mother died believes that my mother had a black child, she even maintains my mother was seen with it.

Well if she did have this child Social Services have no record of it, it had to be born after September 1963 and as she was allegedly seen at the address with it, I can only assume it belonged to someone else, but most definitely not a child my mother gave birth to, so let's put that one to bed forever.

And finally to conclude this episode, my mother it seems had no idea my father was seeing someone else, how do I know this? One night whilst my father's girlfriend was sitting in the local public house (the same pub we held our wedding reception at) my mother walked in, sat down beside her and quite naively, not knowing who she was, said to her, "You don't know who this woman is my Joe's seeing do you?" She always called him "Joe" (short for Josiah). To which the reply came, "No sorry". I'm also not sure if the girlfriend knew who my mother was, but I can imagine her fear if she had (I believe my father had been seeing this new lady in his life for some time, I remember visiting the house where she lived, especially one Christmas Day).

A few weeks or months later it appears my mother found out who she was and where she lived, she went round to the house and forced her way in, looking to find the woman in question. Fortunately she was out but my mother smashed the house up and the police were called. Not the actions of someone who has been estranged for some time. Maybe she was jealous? But then I have to think, jealous of what, if they had not been seeing each other? My father fearing for the safety of his girlfriend and their child decided to move away from the area and moved to Birmingham to a little bedsit in Digbeth. I visited him there on one occasion, having to catch a bus there and back.

I think when my father moved to Birmingham that was the last time he saw my mother, but still he left her with a parting gift, I'll explain later.

There they stayed until he moved down to South Wales where they lived in a caravan, as part of his work down there. You may recall earlier I said that Stephen and Sandra were living down in Pontypridd with them? This is because when Stephen left school and needed to find a job, my father invited him down to Wales to work with him.

My aunt Joan, (my father's sister), who Stephen was living with from 1963, still expected him to pay board to her, ('board' is a fee paid usually to the parents for food, washing etc,) as she put it, "I am keeping your bed for you." So she expected him to pay for his food and lodgings at Pontypridd and pay again up in Dudley! Stephen objected to this, they had words and she threw him out, so ended the fostering period and no more money!

Stephen and Sandra both ended up living down at Pontypridd in separate accommodation to my father and his family, Stephen continuing to work with his father, until Stephen and Sandra returned to Dudley some time later.

So, back to David. Once again I had very little information to go on, I had received the Social Services report detailing David's birth. I had a copy of his original birth certificate telling me where he was born, the date of registration and the address of my mother when she registered the birth. All of the birth certificates allowed me to track my mother's movements over a given period of time.

As the family began to grow we had more resources to throw at this project, resources in relation to the number of people available to carry out certain tasks, such as looking up information, speaking to Social Services etc.

We decided to try a different approach in an attempt to find David. We had originally been to Social Services, which led to the meeting with Thomas and we then enlisted the services of a genealogist to find Mark. It was during the journey to find Mark and the conversations we had with Christine that began to give us an insight into adoptions, adoption procedures and the legislation surrounding children put up for adoption.

We began to understand and get a feeling for the policies and procedures involved in court processes and how children moved through the system. We began to see how entries were placed into the adoption registers and how if you had sufficient knowledge you could second guess when a small baby might have been put up for adoption.

So we started to put a plan together. We knew when David had been born and where. We took a gamble that as Thomas and Mark had been adopted fairly locally and through local courts it made perfect sense that the same thing would have happened to David, that he too would have moved through local courts and been fostered, then later adopted to a local family.

So if we knew the systems and we knew how to access them, why didn't we have a go at trying to find David ourselves? That's exactly what we decided to do. In May 2004 during the spring bank holiday, the 14th I believe, we agreed to go down to London and spend a couple of days searching the records.

Thomas, Tracy, Diane and I booked into a hotel in Knightsbridge. Mark and Susan could only get the one day off work, they agreed to follow us down the following day and join up with us.

The four of us travelled down on the train and arrived around lunch time, we booked in and set about making the short journey over to the Family Records Centre where the registers where kept. It was fairly close to the hotel so we decided to walk it. When we arrived there Thomas, Tracy and Diane and I set about our master plan. Tracy had some searching to do herself in order to find relatives of her own, so she set about that joining us periodically to check on progress.

We had decided that as David had been born in June 1965 so he would possibly have been put up for adoption from 1966 onwards. It was a gamble but if it had been earlier, we could always go backwards. We decided to split the work between us, each searching a specific register, so then we began looking through the adopted children's registers from 1966 onwards.

Now these registers are not a single register for each year, there are four registers for each year, four quarters and they are massive heavy books, approximately 3ft by 2ft by four inches thick, with hundreds of entries on each page. So we began the long arduous search for a male born in the Dudley area, adopted from 1966 onwards and hopefully with the name of David.

It really is like looking for a needle in a haystack, but we continued throughout the day, taking regular breaks in order to rest our eyes. At the end of the day we had reached somewhere around the 'S' in the registers, they go in alphabetical order, and still no success. We had come across a couple of entries but they failed to deliver, the one was from Scotland.

We decided to call it a day and return to the hotel, we had a shower and went down for our evening meal, then spent the evening discussing the day's events and the work Tracy had accomplished, a few drinks later and more reminiscing we retired to bed ready for day two.

The following day, I think this was a Friday we were joined by Mark and Susan and after consuming a fantastic full English breakfast at a little cafe we found (the hotel was too expensive for our tastes), we all made our way to the records office, where once again we began our search.

We picked up from where we left off moving through the registers, carefully examining each entry and with each name and location wondering if we would ever find the relevant entry. We had to accept that he may not have been adopted until much later on, in which case we may well have had to have returned at a later date, noting where we had got to.

We had found a couple of entries and decided to save time it would be a good idea if a couple of us looked these up in the marriage indexes. Once again we had to assume that David had got married and decide on a relevant period in the future when the marriage took place. We were attempting to match the name with a marriage in the Dudley or surrounding area, not very scientific but it works.

We made an educated guess that we would look from an age of about twenty and move forward. We left Mark and Susan to carry on the search through the adopted children's indexes. Both of these entries didn't give us anything to shout about, again they showed marriages in different parts of the country and I had a gut feeling that like the other two David was local.

We decided to go back across the offices and rejoin Mark and Susan, when we got to them, Mark exclaimed he had come across a David Trevor and the information suggested this could be worth following up. The irony was we had been there all day the day before and here was Mark and Susan finding an entry almost without effort! It should be said however, they began their search from the letter 'S' where we had left off the following day, they got to 'W'.

We decided to follow this one up through the marriage index and things now began to get exciting. This entry tied up with a marriage when this particular fellow was thirty and the ceremony took place in Dudley. So we had a boy adopted when he was about two, in Dudley, married when he was thirty, in Dudley and with the same Christian name, both Christian names.

This could all have been a wasted journey, a red herring and a false trail but we had to follow this up, nothing ventured, nothing gained. The one thing we had going for us was the fact that this particular entry indicated that this boy had retained both his Christian names.

We decided to make a note of the entries in both the adopted children's register and the marriage register. We would apply for the adopted birth certificate whilst we were there, it was possible by paying a little extra to get this through to us by 4pm that afternoon.

We decided to wait at the family centre until the certificate was ready, we were waiting for one vital piece of information from this piece of paper – we were waiting with bated breath and anticipation that this certificate would have the same date of birth as David's, if it did not we would have to continue searching at a later date. If it did match, then almost certainly but with still a little apprehension until we could check it further, this could be David our brother.

The time was moving on as we all kept looking at each other, walking the floor like parents in a maternity ward, wondering what was about to befall us, was this what we had all been waiting for, or would it be a big disappointment?

I kept thinking as those minutes ticked past had we followed the correct procedure? Had we done this right, had we moved too quickly, been too impatient and got the whole process wrong?

The time was getting nearer for Mark and Susan to be leaving us, they had travelled down to London by coach and had to make their way back to the coach station via the underground so as not to miss the pickup time. If this certificate was not forthcoming soon they would have to wait a little longer for the answers. Then as the clock ticked closer and closer, one of us and I don't know which one went to ask if it was ready. It was!

It was handed over in a brown envelope, it was like I was about to get the results of a very important exam, I just did not want to be the one to open it, I walked some distance away. One of the others did and I remember quite distinctly looking at the faces of everyone else, to see if I could second guess the result, to see if there was elation or disappointment on their faces.

I can't recall who actually read the certificate, I have a notion it might have been Thomas, everyone else apart from me huddled around him, looking over his shoulder, trying to get a glimpse, and there it was, the adopted birth certificate of David and the **matching** date of birth. The correct day, the correct month and, of course, the correct year.

We now had much more information including the address at which David was living when the adoption took place, and the adopted parents' names. This was never an absolute certainty, we could be looking at a total coincidence and we understood this. We now needed to apply for the marriage certificate so that we would hopefully have a new address for David and his wife.

It was far too late to order the certificate in London, so we decided to return home, take a break and in the cold light of day re-examine all the evidence we had. The train journey back home was far more exciting than the one down. We were all so thrilled at our discovery and I think more so in the fact that we had actually achieved so much ourselves, what a wonderful achievement, if this was indeed our baby brother.

When we got back home I was tasked with ordering the marriage certificate, and I decided not to ask for it to be delivered to me, but I would go down to the registrar of births, deaths and marriages myself and collect it, far quicker that way. So this is what I set about doing. The anticipation was incredible and eventually the certificate of marriage was ready so I went to collect it.

The details gave us an address for David, the name of his wife (Alison) and his father and mother's occupation at the time of the wedding, as well as his age at the time he married. The next step was to try and find a telephone number. The phone book was the obvious choice, a quick look for the surname and tie this in to the address and there it was!

Now all seems very simple at this stage. We are fairly certain this is David, our brother, we have both the original and adopted birth certificates and his marriage certificate, in fact, we probably have more than he himself has. We have his address and contact telephone number, "Simple," I hear you say, "What are you waiting for? Ring it!"

That's exactly what I wanted to do, but what if he had not been told he was adopted? What if I ring the house and his wife answers? What if I ring the house and he answers? I have to tell them who I am, I have to tell them who I am looking for. I could say I'm doing a piece of research for a client who has been adopted and believes the family lived at this address and could they confirm if they have any knowledge of an adoption in the family?

All sounds a bit long winded and what if they say, yes I was adopted or, yes my husband was adopted, what then? This is where we were going into uncharted waters, this was completely new to us and we could cause so much damage if he was unaware of the adoption. Can you imagine being told at thirty the parents who have brought you up all your life are not your real mother and father?

This was a decision I was not prepared to make on my own, so I called Thomas and went to his house that afternoon. We mulled over the dilemma, we looked at every possible scenario and then made our decision, we would make the call, or rather I would make the call.

We went over every possible way of saying what we wanted to say in order to get the message over. I remember saying to Thomas, "I'll ring up and say my name and ask if they have any knowledge of an adoption." I remember Thomas saying perhaps you shouldn't give your name! And I said I have to tell them who I am, you really should have been there that afternoon, it was quite funny when I look back on it!

Anyway with my heart in my mouth I picked up the phone, dialled the number and waited. The call was answered by a woman, I can't fully recall the extent of the conversation, I believe I gave my name and said I'd been searching for my family for quite some time and that I'd managed to find a couple of brothers and my research had led me to this telephone call today.

I remember thinking at some point in the conversation, I am beginning to ramble on here! What must this woman think of me? I had visions of her holding the phone at arm's length thinking, who is this nutcase? I recall thinking I need to ask the vital question, "I believe my brother could be your husband David, do you know if he was adopted?"

However, when I said "I believe my brother could be your husband," she replied, "I think he probably is!" She went on to say that David did indeed know he was adopted and he had been told some years previously that his family name was the same as ours. She had heard or seen the family surname on a piece of paper or birth certificate, so she was fairly sure about the connection to her husband.

This was far too much of a coincidence, the chances of us having come across two individuals almost with identical pasts, with identical dates of birth, identical surnames at the time of adoption were too spooky to even contemplate, besides the Social Service records tied everything together.

I was talking to my brother's wife 'Alison'. We had found David! I went on to ask Alison if David would want to meet us? She stated that he had actually started to look for his family a couple of years earlier, but due to family issues he decided to leave things at that point and had not mentioned it since. So once again it was left to the wife to break the good news to her husband. I left my phone number with Alison to hand to David and asked her to ask him to call me that evening.

I put the phone down, put my arms around Thomas and we both cried. I went home, called Stephen and Mark to tell them the good news and waited yet again for a phone call.

Alison tells me that when David arrived home from work that evening she was so much in shock at what had happened she just did not know how to tell him, she was not sure how he might react. They were looking after a friend's house and had to feed the fish that night, so Alison delayed as much as she dared and after they had been back from the friend's house for about an hour she told David to sit down, she told him she had something to tell him.

Now once again, put yourself in David's shoes, your wife has been fairly quiet, you sense there is something not quite right and she then tells you to sit down to break some news to you. His first reaction was, Alison was pregnant, to which she said "No!", his second reaction was, she was about to tell him she was having an affair, to which again she said "No!". The poor bloke was running out of options, what on earth could this news be?

She came right out with it and told him she had received a phone call earlier in the day and it was from one of his brothers called John. She went on to explain what I had said and gave him my phone number.

She tells me he was extremely quiet for some time and then began to cry. It wasn't long thereafter he called me and once again the emotions, the tears and above all the elation of being able to talk to my baby brother for the first time in my life was overwhelming.

During all these initial calls from Thomas, Mark and David, I came off the phone so full of disbelief at what was happening to me and falling into the arms of my wife and sobbing uncontrollably, time after time.

What a wonderful feeling!

My children also shared my happiness with me, they thought it was great that at last I was finding my long lost family, a family I had often talked to them about, a family that up to recently had only been evident on Social Service records or a distant memory.

It was decided that on this occasion Thomas, Mark, Stephen and I would meet David on our own at a local pub, which is precisely what we did a couple or so nights later. Once again we waited until his arrival and in turn we all gave him a big hug. This meeting would, I imagine, have been more difficult for David than anyone of us. We had already been through this process and met each other, first Thomas, Stephen and I, and then Thomas, Stephen and I met Mark.

Here was David having to meet all four of us, but that's the way he wanted to do it, he didn't want to meet us separately, he wanted to see us all at the same time. That evening we talked and we asked one of the waitresses in the pub to take a photograph of the five of us, all of us still have that photo of the first time we were all together in our entire lives.

David explained to us that he was aware he had a biological family and knew he had indeed been adopted. He told us of his life during this spell and unlike the life Thomas and Mark had experienced, David's life was not so happy or contented, he later found some solitude in the comfort and love of Alison.

A week or so later we all met up at Thomas's house, this was May 2004. David would be thirty-nine the following month. David, unlike the others, never had the opportunity to meet his biological father he had passed away some four years earlier, this event didn't go without controversy.

My father had been ill for quite some time following a heart bypass he never seemed to recover from. Eventually, following periods of hospital admissions and tests, me and his new family, his wife, son and two daughters were called to the hospital. It was there in a side room we were to be told, with my father present, that he had cancer situated behind his heart and it was inoperable. I recall for the first time in my life my father cried.

A few weeks later in November, I was called by his daughter to attend the hospital where he had been admitted earlier and told to hurry, that his time was limited. I called Stephen, arranged to pick him up and called the others, Thomas and Mark.

When I arrived at his bedside, apart from his wife and three children, also present were his two sisters, Joan and Sylvia. I stood at the foot of the bed for perhaps ten minutes looking at him with his head to one side, then he turned his head towards me, looked at me and I said, "It's ok dad you can go now." He took one last breath and left this world behind.

Left to right, back row: Diane, Me, Sandra, Steve, David, Alison.
Front row: Thomas, Tracy, Mark, Susan.

Thomas and Mark arrived a few minutes later and went in to say their goodbyes, we all moved into a side room to compose ourselves and later the nurse came in to ask who she needed to talk to concerning my father. You would have thought that this would have been his wife, however, she was extremely deaf and therefore, as I was the eldest child it would have been me. And I was just about to open my mouth when Joan or Sylvia very quickly interjected, "That will be Maxine." (My father's daughter, my stepsister).

Once again me and Stephen were pushed to one side. But do you know, at that moment it really didn't matter, my father had gone, my mother long before, but I had my brothers beside me.

I turned to Stephen and said, "Time for us to leave." We went home.

We attended our father's funeral a while later and said goodbye, occasionally I visit the grave, just so he knows I have not forgotten him, a promise I made to his brother, my uncle Jim, on the day of the funeral.

Now that both my parents were dead I was ready to get on with a project I had promised myself to complete. For many years I had thought of writing down my experiences and the journey I had made from childhood to adulthood, I wanted to write a book!

The reason I delayed writing was due to a conversation Stephen and I had with my father many years before. We were sitting in a pub having a drink, talking about finding the "kids", when my father said, "There are things I will take to my grave." I never challenged him about that statement, for I knew he would not elaborate, however, I recall thinking at that moment there can't be much he knows that I don't know.

Perhaps I was being naive, but I was there right up until the separation, I saw what was going on, I heard what was going on, was very much a part of it and most important of all, I remembered it.

It was then I decided to wait and get as much information as I could before making the decision to put pen to paper. If there was something in the past he wanted left there, but I was privy to it, I felt it wasn't my place to bring it to the forefront while he was alive.

During these fragmented periods of thought and reflection I began to wonder why my father had never filed for divorce and why, when my mother died did he return to Dudley? Was his justification for remaining married due to the probability he would have to find and make contact with my mother in filing for divorce? I can understand his reasoning for not doing that. When he did return to Dudley he lived in a house on a local council estate, there he had two more children, three in total and lived his second life with the woman who eventually became my stepmother.

Stephen and I would visit them occasionally and he would visit us, bringing with him our step siblings. We got on with our lives and were quite amicable.

There was one more journey to take, one more sibling to find to complete my family.

It was now time to move on and search for Susan.

Phew!!!

ELEVEN

Susan

THIS SEARCH was to be completely different, but then what was new? We would come across situations alien to us and difficult to comprehend, we came across a document relating to legislation that meant we had to make a decision, do we plod on in the dark or do we wait before beginning our search in earnest?

The Adoption and Children Act 2002 represented the most radical overhaul of adoption law for 26 years, replacing the outdated Adoption Act 1976 and modernising the entire legal framework for domestic and intercountry adoption. It brought in many changes that were intended to help improve adoption services for children and their families by birth and adoption. For the first time, the legislation recognised the needs of birth relatives who want the opportunity to let their adult adopted relative know of their interest for contact.

This piece of legislation had the potential of opening doors for us.

Under Section 98 of the Adoption and Children Act 2002 (England and Wales), birth relatives of an adopted adult, and adopted people themselves, have the legal right to ask a local authority, voluntary adoption agency or adoption support agency that has registered as an intermediary agency to provide them with intermediary services so that their adopted relatives or birth relatives know of their wish for communication and contact. Agencies that provide intermediary services must give priority to those adoptions that took place on or before the 12th November 1975.

Susan was born before this date so the wheels began to turn, the brain cogs were going full speed and we saw more potential. This new law came into effect on 30th December 2005 and was to play a significant part in our search.

There is no statutory requirement for adoption agencies to provide an intermediary service but there is a requirement on those who hold adoption records to provide information to intermediary agencies. If the adoption agency you approach cannot provide you with a service, it will point you to an agency that can.

Although some adoption agencies have provided intermediary services for birth relatives for many years, the availability and the extent of the services offered has remained something of a postcode lottery. There has also been inconsistent practice and no national regulated standards and safeguards. The changes to the law have therefore been welcomed by many of those affected by adoption and adoption specialists, as it means that all people will be able to access a service, regardless of where they live.

Again, this was falling into place, had we found a new avenue? So, with all this information at our fingertips and given our recent experiences and successes, we thought long and hard as to the best approach in searching for Susan.

We had her birth name, which strangely in comparison with all the other children my mother had given birth to was a single name, all the others including myself had two Christian names. So if we had chosen to search the adoption records as we did with David, we were looking for a girl with the possibility of retaining her birth name, we felt this was unlikely and would therefore prove extremely difficult.

I knew from the records I had seen at Monyhull during the interview I had with a Dr Freedman in November 1986, that my mother had arrived in Birmingham and had been befriended by a man named Campbell. She was admitted to Monyhull on 23rd October 1967 and Susan was born one month later at the maternity hospital. Records show that Susan was taken to Dr Hudson's Homes, later Susan was adopted and no further information was known.

When we began to look into this report more closely we began to see the glaring errors. Apart from the fact that the information they had on record was wholly incorrect, including the order of the children's births, the fact they had missed Michael's birth and had Stephen as second eldest.

They had the third child recorded as having died, when in fact the third child was Stephen and he was very much alive. They had completely missed David off the list, I assume they had extracted this information from my mother, demonstrating her confusion at the time. They certainly had not received it from Dudley Social Services. Had we have followed these records heaven knows where we would have got to and we would certainly not have found David.

The other confusing piece of information was related to Dr Hudson Homes. When we searched we found no such agency, Father Hudson yes, but surely such an organisation as large as a hospital, part of the regional N.H.S would not make such a glaring mistake? Maybe, just maybe, they meant Dr Barnardo's?

So during the middle part of 2004, whilst we waited for the new legislation to kick in through December 2005, we began to send out letters to both these societies in the hope that one of them had handled or, at the very least had some information, relating to Susan's adoption or aftercare.

During May and June I received two letters back from Father Hudson's & Barnardo's saying they were very sorry but they had no record of Susan. It was now beginning to look like someone somewhere had either accidentally or deliberately lost her records, mislaid them or had not recorded her whereabouts following her birth at the maternity hospital.

So logically you would think here is a child born to a woman who has just been admitted to a hospital for the mentally subnormal. They may not be aware at this point that she has had seven previous children of which three have been adopted and two taken into care. However, being a resident of Monyhull she would not have been allowed to take the baby there when she went back following the birth. So you would think the hospital would have contacted Social Services, explained the situation, Social Services would then take the child into care, possible foster the child out with a view to adoption later on? That's what we thought! So writing to Birmingham Social Services and asking for information should get some sort of response.

Whilst we waited, I wrote to numerous adoption agencies, charities involved in adoption and Social Service departments within local councils across the country. All came back with a similar response, "Sorry" unable to trace any records relating to your sister, please try other agencies etc. Every time a letter came through the door I hoped and prayed that this would be the one that said, "Yes" we have a record of your sister.

But it never happened, as each one fell to the floor and I opened it my heart sank yet again. Was this going to be the pattern? Were we doomed to failure?

Then in January 2006 I received a letter from Birmingham Social Services, surely this was to be the one that would unlock the door to the path of reconciliation? They suggested I contact Adoption Support, an adoption support services agency, as they themselves did not provide this kind of service.

Once again I began to think I was being 'fobbed off', that they just didn't realise how important this was to us all. However, if they didn't provide such a service then I needed to contact this agency in order to move things on. So I wrote yet another letter to a support agency asking for any assistance or guidance in finding our sister. This is when the new legislation kicked in and it seemed to me many months later, that we were being led down a particular path by a force unknown to us.

It was now January 2006, one month after the legislation came into force. I received a letter from the adoption support agency stating that because Susan was born in Birmingham there was a possibility that Birmingham Social Services handled the adoption, at my request they could ask Social Services to forward the file if they held it. They could not, however, hand over any identifying information contained within the file to me or any other member of the birth family.

Once the file is received they check it to make sure it is the correct file and then allocate an adoption support worker who then prepares non-identifying information from the file and arranges an appointment. They then need to carry out research to find Susan. So yes, we said please go ahead and sent a cheque for £75 to cover the cost of research.

We quickly learnt that Birmingham City Council did not hold a file on Susan and therefore resigned ourselves to the possibility of disappointment. Another year passed by with telephone calls back and forth, requesting a little more information and me asking for updates.

In January 2007 I received a call from the adoption support worker saying they now had a possible address and a name, she said they were fairly confident due to the fact that Susan's new surname was unusual. I must admit at that point I was very intrigued and I was then offered by letter a couple of appointments to choose from, to go to Birmingham to discuss my request to trace Susan.

So on Wednesday 31st January at 2pm I arrived at the adoption support agency in Birmingham. It was here I was informed that although Birmingham did not hold a file on Susan, the adoption agency had contacted the General Registrar Office and requested three pieces of information; the agency or court that handled Susan's adoption, the adopted name, the parents name and address.

They then began a search and were now in a position to confirm to me the following, they told me they had found Susan, her name had obviously changed and she was now named Tania! She had indeed been adopted from a young age and had been privately adopted to a couple living in Birmingham.

I was informed that her mother was a former psychiatric nurse and her father was a Chinese fellow, hence her unusual name. For confidentiality reasons I won't mention it here, but it contains just two letters.

On February 14th, of all days, she called the adoption agency and she was thrilled at the thought we had been looking for her. It transpired that she herself had begun a search for her biological mother (our mother) some time back, but circumstances prevailing at the time meant she had to put things on hold.

She had a family of her own and had moved down to Cardiff, which is where they found her. They suggested I write a letter to her to begin with and she would write back.

So this I did, but attempting to introduce yourself to your sister, a person you have not met, never spoken to and never seen is extremely difficult. How do you start such a letter? What do you say?

I was also very much aware of not saying the wrong thing, something that might inadvertently give her the wrong impression, put her off if you understand? And what is it she would like to know? Anyway I got on with it, I told her she had five brothers, how long we had all been searching for each other and how much we would like to meet her.

I also used my initiative, because I believed in my experience of finding the others and subsequent conversations with them, that she would not be happy or satisfied with letters coming and going. So I suggested to her that if she wanted to talk to me before a prearranged meeting at Birmingham (as the adoption agency had recommended) she could ring the agency and I would be more than happy for them to give her my telephone number. They would not give us her number or address at this point in time.

Well, of course the temptation was too much and the agency called me to say she had been in touch and was it ok to hand over my number? At this point I was again awaiting a telephone call from a sibling, my baby sister whom I had never met, never seen and never spoken to in thirty-nine years.

Guess what, when the call came I cried yet again, but this was to be the final time I would experience this emotion because now, I had found them all. From those early days of wondering, wishing and hoping beyond hope, my dreams had now come true.

This was Tuesday 20th February 2007, 1984, twenty-three years earlier, seemed a long way away. We talked about my family, her family, her children and her early life. We agreed not to meet in Birmingham as had been suggested, Tania wanted to meet us all together.

So Saturday 5th May 2007, was to be a monumental day in my life, this was the day Tania came up to visit for a weekend. This day was the first time it became possible for all six of us to be together since 1967, 40 years.

We all met up at my place and waited with bated breath for her to arrive, as with the other reunions we had no idea what to expect, but as with the other reunions we were not disappointed. We spent most of the Saturday exchanging thoughts and experiences, attempting as far as is possible to catch up.

But having to come to terms with once again, the fact that all those years are gone, lost forever, there are no memories for us as individuals to relate to in terms of us being together as brothers and sister when we were children. We can't in our conversations say, "Do you remember when we did that?"

Our lives here and now are what are important, that we do not lose sight of what we have and what we have achieved together.

We continue to meet on occasions, some of us more than others, but isn't that typical of all families? We tend to arrange to be together at Christmas or the New Year, we are conscious of not meeting as often as perhaps we should, but then, I tend to think that this is because of all the years we have not been together, we believe in our subconscious we need to be together more.

We realise and understand there are other commitments and that if we do need each other we are a phone call away. The one underlying fact is, we all love each other and are not afraid to say it, we lost too much time all those years ago, can never retrieve it and must therefore hold fast to the gift we have, the gift of family.

From the year I was born in 1955 to Susan's (Tania's) birth in 1967, there spans just 12 years, almost 13. During this epoch my mother had eight children, two deceased and four adopted. If circumstances had been different we would perhaps have been brought up together, excluding Michael we may have lived our lives alongside Karen.

Would we be any different to the way we are now? If fate plays a part in our life's journey then I believe "Yes" we would. For the others, Stephen, Thomas, Mark, David and Susan I can't speak, but for me? Had I have remained with my mother and father I would not have gone to live with my aunt Alice and uncle Jack. My father would not have moved me to my grandparents and I would not have met my wife, I would not have the children and grandchildren I have now.

So, would I want to change anything? Would I want to go back and make things different? No, sorry! The life I have now is enriched and blessed and there is one solitary event that changed my life forever, the one event that gave me reason and justification to become the person I am today and that was meeting my wife, she was as I have already said the first person to tell me she loved me. She has become the only person in my life I can confide in, share my pain, my thoughts, my disappointments, my joy and elation. She is my life breath.

She gives me strength and reason and much more, and because of that I accept that my life was destined to be different to that of many other children, but as an adult and a man I have the ability to bring about change, I have control now over how I live my life and the path I choose.

The journey I chose and the decisions I made have led me to finding my family and I would not want to change a single event, because changing one event has cause and effect on another.

So we move on, we live our separate lives as individuals with families of our own. We are thankful that our children bring new life into our lives and their children eventually doing the same.

Had I not begun this journey all those years ago my family would be 21 strong. Today it consists of 43. When I set out to find Thomas I also found a further 21 family members, and it will continue to grow.

I love my life, I love my family.

TWELVE

Future

THE PAST has gone only memories remain like waves on a beach, each one bringing something new, then disappearing and leaving behind something to treasure and something to look forward to. The future is what we make of it and what we make of it is our future.

So what of us? The adults we have become, where are we now?

Well for myself, I came through my childhood and became the first one in my family to go to University, three years at Brunel, completing my employment as a principal officer with the local authority, ironically, working with families living in deprivation, using my skills and experiences to help them overcome their difficulties.

There were those I came into contact with who had suffered or were suffering family breakdowns, separation and uncertainty in their lives. They would say to me, "I know you're only trying to help, but you don't understand." And I would say, "Actually I do understand, for I have been where you have been and I have felt what you have felt, but with the right guidance and belief that you will come through this, there is light at the end of the tunnel, but it has to come from you, from within. Believe that there is another way, and life can be better."

My employment has included, apart from engineering, selling double glazing, retail management and merchandising for a large scale retail chain. I'm now happy, contented and fulfilled, I have four sons, four grandsons and two granddaughters. Oh yes, how could I possibly forget, one of my grandsons continues the Fisher family tradition – his name is 'J' Fisher!

Stephen has worked all of his life and lives happily with his wife and family, two sons and one daughter, spending time with his grandchildren, two grandsons and one granddaughter, running his grandsons football team amongst other things. His wife and daughter work in the care sector looking after the needs of others. Stephen is very much a family man, not afraid to challenge those who might question him or stand in his way, a passive man in many ways, but will lose his temper if pushed.

Thomas has his own business and recently built his own house, his wife works with children and young people with special needs within a children's centre. Thomas is very similar to me in character. He is a wise, intelligent man who thinks things through before acting, he has a dry sense of humour and can be very witty at times, the only unfortunate thing about Thomas is he supports Aston Villa! He has one daughter and one son, who have blessed him with two grandsons and two granddaughters.

Mark works in the Health and Safety sector as a trainer, working towards further qualifications. Mark is the comedian of the family, he once turned up at a family fancy dress party dressed in boxer shorts and an 'apron' as the naked chef. Mark is a skilled and highly qualified martial arts practitioner and he continues to study very hard in order to better himself and he will. Mark has two daughters.

David has worked with Stephen. David is the quiet man of the family, he doesn't say a lot but when he does it's worth listening to. David, like me, has not had it so good during his life and there are things remembered that are best forgotten. But he too has fought adversity and triumphed, he has a wonderful wife and children to be proud of. David has a son and daughter.

And as for our Tania? Tania is very much like my mother, in her traits only. She knows what she wants and she gets it, I would not like to get into an argument with her! She spends most of her time looking after her grandchildren and she is an accomplished chef. She has three sons, one daughter and five grandchildren.

I'd like to conclude this journey with a couple of letters, a poem and a song. This letter is from David, written shortly after we met him, I know he won't mind me sharing it with you:

Dear John,

How do I say "thank you" to a brother that's spent his life bringing his family together? Knowing we were all out there somewhere. Not knowing if we were alive or dead. You cared enough to look and find out and thanks to your persistence you found us.

You will never know how proud I am of you, you're a very special man, I couldn't have wished for a better big brother. I have spent most of my life knowing there was something missing, then you all came along and suddenly my life made sense.

You accepted me unconditionally and welcomed me into the family as the youngest brother, it felt scary, emotional but above all, wonderful. I simply want to say "thank you" to you John, Diane and all my family, I know you all had a part to play in making my life complete.

I love you very much and feel very proud to have a brother like you, a family like ours, which is now whole. I have finally accepted that we cannot dwell on the past, we can't change it, but we can decide our future, my future is with my family.

With all my love, always,

David.

This is a card sent to me from Tania following her first visit to us:

To, Diane, John and Stephen,

This is a big thank you for bringing all our family together. All my life I have longed to fit in and when I was with you all at the weekend, for the first time in my life I felt I did.

My mom and dad couldn't have left me with anything better than my brothers and I will always love them for that.

I believe I have dad's looks and mom's personality, for which I wouldn't have got through the last forty years without.

Love you all very much, see you soon.

Love you,

Sis Tania.

Xx

And a poem sent to me from Tania's daughter, Mariah, aged 11

> To my uncle John
> we've a whole new life ahead of us
> something we never knew
> our family has extended
> we now have all of you
> I'm happy for my mom
> and also for us too
> I'm nervous but excited
> I can't wait to meet all of you.

During Boxing Day 2009 we were all invited to join Thomas and his family at his home. During the evening, Stephen gave all the brothers and Tania a CD, called "When I look at you" by Jane McDonald. Stephen had written on each one, "I heard this and thought of us all together at last". In order to appreciate this you need to listen to it, something I can't do here, however, here are the lyrics:

> When I look at you
> you take me back a thousand years
> somewhere in another time, another sphere
> the memory's clear, even now
>
> And when I look at you
> I see a place where I belong
> somewhere in the past
> where I was young and strong
> a long, a long time ago
>
> I always knew that you
> someday you'd find me
> through the test of time
> you'd find me
> follow piece of mind
> and you'd be here with me

I've waited all my life
to say I love you
every hour each day I've loved you
words, can never really say
what's in my Heart

Now, when I look at you
I feel the power all around
looking back into your eyes
I know I've found
a higher ground within my soul

And when I look at you
a Highest Mountain I can climb
knowing that I love you till
the end of time
you know your mine for ever more.

So I hope you have enjoyed sharing my journey, my life, and my experiences and if you have any brothers or sisters who you may be aware are adopted and if you wondered what your brother or sister might be doing right now, where they are, what they are like, what happened to them? Then I hope the information I have been able to give and the journey and adventure I embarked upon will help you on your journey to finding them. If not, at least to know they are well and happy! But beware of sitting there wondering, they might be doing the same thing. Such a waste! Be inspired! I have been fortunate I found Thomas and the rest of my siblings.

So finally!

My last words are for you Mom.

"All your babies are back together.
Rest in peace! I love you."
Your son John.

X

Remember:

Most of the important things in the world have been accomplished by people who have kept on trying when there seemed to be no hope at all.
— Dale Carnegie

Thomas, Stephen, David, Tania, Mark, John – all together.

My Family Tree

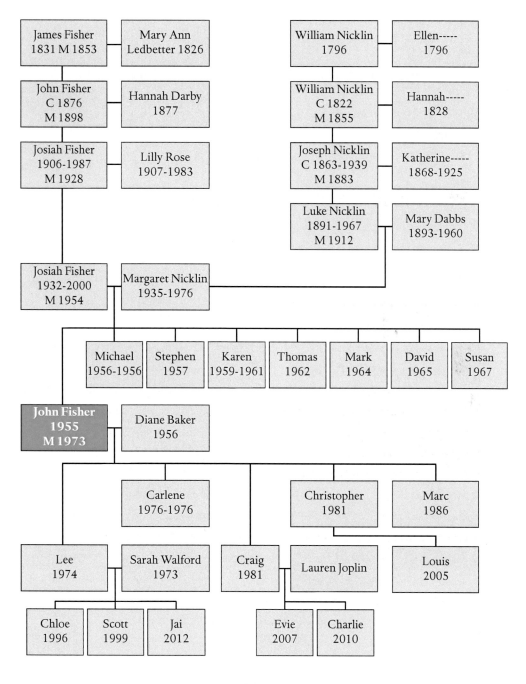

| James Fisher 1831 M 1853 | Mary Ann Ledbetter 1826 | | William Nicklin 1796 | Ellen----- 1796 |

| John Fisher C 1876 M 1898 | Hannah Darby 1877 | | William Nicklin C 1822 M 1855 | Hannah----- 1828 |

| Josiah Fisher 1906-1987 M 1928 | Lilly Rose 1907-1983 | | Joseph Nicklin C 1863-1939 M 1883 | Katherine----- 1868-1925 |

| Luke Nicklin 1891-1967 M 1912 | Mary Dabbs 1893-1960 |

| Josiah Fisher 1932-2000 M 1954 | Margaret Nicklin 1935-1976 |

| Michael 1956-1956 | Stephen 1957 | Karen 1959-1961 | Thomas 1962 | Mark 1964 | David 1965 | Susan 1967 |

| John Fisher 1955 M 1973 | Diane Baker 1956 |

| Carlene 1976-1976 | Christopher 1981 | Marc 1986 |

| Lee 1974 | Sarah Walford 1973 | Craig 1981 | Lauren Joplin | Louis 2005 |

| Chloe 1996 | Scott 1999 | Jai 2012 | Evie 2007 | Charlie 2010 |

My Mom